D0508245

Ready, Steady, Spaghetti

cooking for kids and with kids

Ready, Steady, Spaghetti

cooking for kids and with kids

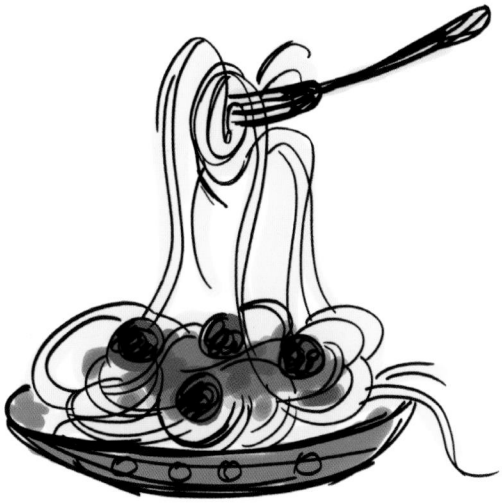

Lucy Broadhurst

whitecap

contents

read this first... 6

little food 8

dinner time 38

eat your greens 84

sticky puddings 100

biscuits, cakes and fetes 126

let's party! 154

index 188

read this first...

Cooking is great fun but, before you rush into the kitchen, take a bit of time to get organized. There aren't many rules to cooking but there is a golden one: always read RIGHT TO THE END OF THE RECIPE before you start. Can you imagine how annoying it would be to get to step 4 of your recipe and then have to bribe your little brother to run to the shops for a missing ingredient? So, read all the way through and get out all the ingredients and equipment you're going to need.

Chop or shred any ingredients you can before you start. Open tins and wash vegetables or fruit. Grease or line any baking tins you're going to need.

When you've been cooking for a while you will be able to estimate quantities fairly accurately, but until then measure carefully, especially when you're baking. You'll see that there are three different scales for measuring: metric, imperial and cup measures, so there should be something to suit every kitchen. A cup measure is a standard 250 ml (9 fl oz). Spoon measures are always level, never heaped (unless the recipe specifically says so).

If you're using the oven, arrange the shelves to the correct height before you turn it on. And preheat it before putting things in to cook — the oven will probably have a light to show when it's reached the right temperature. If you put things in the oven and then switch it on to warm up, the food will dry out, and won't be cooked when the recipe says it should be. If you have a fan-forced oven, the temperature will be a bit hotter than a normal oven. The temperature in the recipes is for a normal oven. If you use fan-forced, you don't need to preheat the oven, but you will need to put the temperature to about 10°C (18°F) lower than the recipe says.

All of the recipes have photographs so you can see what your finished dish is going to look like. Don't worry too much if it doesn't look exactly the same... the taste is what matters, not the appearance! Some recipes have step photographs, too, so you can check any tricky techniques as you go.

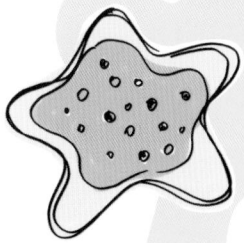

Nutrition

Before you start cooking, it's a good idea to know how food works in your body. There are five different food groups — protein, carbohydrate, fibre, fat, and vitamins and minerals — all of which play different roles. Proteins, such as meat, fish, dairy (cheese, milk and eggs), pulses and nuts, will build your muscles and help you grow. Protein also takes longer to digest, so can keep you feeling full for longer and prevent snacking — that's why it's a good idea to include some protein in your breakfast. Carbohydrates, such as bread, potatoes, rice and pasta, give you energy. Fibre keeps your insides working properly. Fat, in small amounts, is still an important nutrient, especially for bodies that are growing. Fats from oily fish, nuts, seeds, avocado and olive oil are the best fats to include regularly. Eating the right amounts of each group will leave you feeling fit and healthy, with plenty of energy, will help your body to stay at its correct weight and, for children, help your body grow and develop properly. Eating healthily is a matter of following a balanced diet. If you eat three good meals and get vitamins from plenty of fruit and vegetables on most days, then you can afford to indulge in party food on your friends' birthdays.

Hygiene and safety

1 Always ask an adult for permission before you start to cook. And always ask for help if you are not confident with chopping or handling hot pans. An adult must always be present if the recipe involves deep-frying.

2 Before you start, wash your hands well with soap and water, tie back long hair and wear an apron to protect your clothes.

3 When you're cooking on the stovetop, turn pan handles to the side so there's no danger of knocking them as you walk past. When you're stirring, hold the pan handle firmly. Always use thick, dry oven gloves when you're getting things out of the oven.

4 Chicken should be treated with care, as it can harbor salmonella bacteria. Keep it in the fridge for no more than 2 days, or freeze it for up to 6 months. Once you've thawed chicken, you can't freeze it again unless you cook it first. When you've chopped raw chicken, wash the chopping board and knife before you prepare other ingredients that aren't going to be cooked (such as salad ingredients).

5 Wash up as you go along. This will save hours of cleaning at the end and will keep your work space clear.

little food

berry couscous

SERVES 4–6

185 g (6½ oz/1 cup) instant couscous

500 ml (17 fl oz/2 cups) apple and cranberry juice

1 cinnamon stick

250 g (9 oz/2 cups) frozen raspberries, thawed

250 g (9 oz/1⅔ cups) frozen blueberries, thawed

2 teaspoons grated orange zest

250 g (9 oz/1⅔ cups) strawberries, halved

185 g (6½ oz/¾ cup) plain yoghurt

1. Put the couscous in a bowl. Pour the juice in a saucepan and add the cinnamon stick. Cover and bring to the boil. Pour over the couscous.
2. Cover with plastic wrap and leave for about 5 minutes, or until all the liquid has disappeared. Remove the cinnamon stick from the bowl.
3. Gently pat the thawed berries with paper towels to dry them. Fluff the grains of couscous with a fork, then gently fold in the orange zest and most of the berries.
4. Spoon into four serving bowls and sprinkle with the remaining berries. Serve with a dollop of yoghurt.

french toast

SERVES 2

2 eggs
250 ml (9 fl oz/1 cup) milk
1/2 teaspoon vanilla extract
40 g (1 1/2 oz) butter
4 thick slices day-old bread
ground cinnamon and sugar, to serve

1. Break the eggs into a wide shallow dish and add the milk and vanilla extract. Beat with a fork or wire whisk until well mixed.
2. Melt half the butter in a frying pan. When the butter begins to bubble, quickly dip a piece of bread into the egg mixture, let the excess run off, then place it in the pan.
3. Cook for 1–2 minutes. When it is golden underneath, turn the bread over and cook the other side.
4. Transfer the French toast to a plate and cover with foil to keep warm while you cook the rest. Add more butter to the pan as needed and cook the remaining bread. Serve sprinkled with cinnamon and sugar.

ham and corn muffins

MAKES 24

125 g (4½ oz/1 cup) self-raising flour

40 g (1½ oz) ham, chopped

60 g (2¼ oz/⅓ cup) tinned corn kernels, drained

¼ red capsicum (pepper), deseeded and finely chopped

2 teapoons chopped flat-leaf (Italian) parsley

60 g (2¼ oz) unsalted butter, melted

125 ml (4 fl oz/½ cup) milk

1 egg

1 tablespoon sesame seeds

1. Preheat the oven to 210°C (415°F/Gas 6–7). Brush 24 mini muffin holes with oil. Sift the flour into a large bowl. Add the ham, corn, capsicum and parsley and stir to combine.
2. Mix the melted butter, milk and egg in a bowl. Make a well in the centre of the flour mixture and add the milk mixture. Mix the dough lightly until the ingredients are just combined.
3. Spoon the mixture into the muffin holes and sprinkle with the sesame seeds. Bake for 15–20 minutes, or until golden.

berry muffins

MAKES 16

250 g (9 oz/1 cup) plain yoghurt

100 g (3½ oz/1 cup) rolled (porridge) oats

3 tablespoons oil

80 g (2¾ oz/⅓ cup) caster (superfine) sugar

1 egg

125 g (4½ oz/1 cup) self-raising flour, sifted

3 teaspoons baking powder

200 g (7 oz/1⅓ cups) frozen mixed berries, thawed

1. Preheat the oven to 180°C (350°F/Gas 4). Place paper cases into 16 standard muffin holes. Mix the yoghurt, oats, oil, caster sugar and egg in a bowl. Gently stir in the sifted flour and baking powder with the berries.
2. Spoon the mixture into the paper cases. Bake for 20–25 minutes, or until the muffins are golden brown.

blueberry pancakes

MAKES 12

250 g (9 oz/2 cups) plain (all-purpose) flour

2 teaspoons baking powder

1 teaspoon bicarbonate of soda (baking soda)

75 g (2½ oz/⅓ cup) sugar

2 eggs

80 g (2¾ oz) unsalted butter, melted

310 ml (10¾ fl oz/1¼ cups) milk

310 g (11 oz/2 cups) blueberries, fresh or frozen

honey and plain yoghurt, to serve (optional)

1. Sift the flour, baking powder and bicarbonate of soda into a large bowl. Add the sugar and make a well in the centre. Add the eggs, melted butter and milk to the dry ingredients, stirring just to combine (add more milk if you prefer a thinner batter).
2. Gently fold the blueberries into the batter (leave some for serving). Heat a frying pan and brush lightly with melted butter or oil. Drop tablespoons of batter into the pan and cook over low heat until bubbles appear and pop on the surface.
3. Turn the pancakes over and cook the other side (these pancakes can be difficult to handle so take care when turning). Transfer to a plate and cover with a cloth to keep warm while you cook the rest of the batter. Serve warm with some blueberries, a drizzle of honey and plain yoghurt, if using.

scrambled eggs

SERVES 2

4 eggs

3 tablespoons milk

15 g (1/2 oz) butter

toast or English muffins, to serve

1. Beat the eggs and milk lightly with a fork.
2. Melt the butter in a heavy-based frying pan over very low heat and pour in the egg. Stir constantly with a wooden spoon, lifting the mixture from the bottom of the pan so that it cooks evenly. The eggs are ready when they are just set but are still creamy.
3. Remove from the heat and serve immediately on toast or English muffins.

hummus

SERVES 4

220 g (7 3/4 oz/1 cup) dried chickpeas
4 tablespoons olive oil, plus extra to drizzle
3–4 tablespoons lemon juice
2 garlic cloves, crushed
2 tablespoons tahini
1 tablespoon ground cumin
crackers, to serve

1. Soak the chickpeas in water for 8 hours, or overnight. Drain. Put in a saucepan and cover with cold water. Bring to the boil and cook for 50–60 minutes. Drain, keeping a cupful of the cooking liquid.
2. Put the chickpeas in a food processor with the oil, lemon juice, garlic, tahini and cumin. Blend well until the mixture starts to look thick and creamy. With the motor running, gradually add the cooking liquid until the mixture is as thick or thin as you like it. Transfer to a bowl and drizzle with olive oil. Serve with crackers, raw or cooked vegetables, or use as a spread for sandwiches.

tzatziki

SERVES 12

2 Lebanese (short) cucumbers
410 g (14 1/2 oz/1 2/3 cups) low-fat plain yoghurt
4 garlic cloves, crushed
3 tablespoons finely chopped mint
1 tablespoon lemon juice
raw vegetables, to serve

1. Cut the cucumbers in half lengthways and scoop out the seeds. Leave the skin on and coarsely grate the cucumbers into a colander. Sprinkle with salt and leave over a large bowl for 15 minutes to drain off any bitter juices.
2. Stir together the yoghurt, garlic, mint and lemon juice in a bowl.
3. Rinse the cucumber under cold water then, taking small handfuls, squeeze out any excess moisture. Mix the grated cucumber with the yoghurt. Serve with raw vegetables.

dhal

SERVES 4–6

310 g (11 oz/1 1/4 cups) red lentils
30 g (1 oz) unsalted butter
1 onion, finely chopped
2 garlic cloves, crushed
1 teaspoon grated fresh ginger
1 teaspoon ground turmeric
1 teaspoon garam masala
pitta bread, to serve

1. Put the lentils in a large bowl and cover with water. Remove any floating particles and drain the lentils.
2. Heat the butter in a saucepan. Fry the onion for about 3 minutes, or until soft. Add the garlic, ginger and spices. Cook, stirring, for 1 minute.
3. Add the lentils and 500 ml (17 fl oz/2 cups) of water and bring to the boil. Lower the heat and simmer, stirring occasionally, for 15 minutes, or until all the water has been absorbed.
4. Transfer to a serving bowl and serve warm with pitta bread.

guacamole

SERVES 4–6

2 avocados
1/2 small red onion, finely chopped
1 tomato, chopped
1 tablespoon lemon juice
3 tablespoons sour cream

1. Cut the avocados in half and remove the stones.
2. Peel the avocados and place the flesh into a bowl. Mash with a fork until smooth.
3. Add the onion, tomato, lemon juice and sour cream. Stir to combine. Serve as a dip with pitta bread, corn chips or nachos.

nachos

SERVES 6–8

440 g (15½ oz) tinned red kidney beans
3 tablespoons oil
1 large onion, peeled and chopped
2 garlic cloves, crushed
2 large ripe tomatoes, chopped
125 g (4½ oz/½ cup) tomato salsa
Tabasco sauce, to taste
750 g (1 lb 10 oz) corn chips
310 g (11 oz/2½ cups) grated cheddar cheese
guacamole and sour cream, to serve

1. Preheat the oven to 180°C (350°F/Gas 4). Rinse the kidney beans in a colander and drain. Mash with a fork.
2. Heat the oil in a frying pan over medium heat and cook the onion and garlic until soft.
3. Add the tomatoes, tomato salsa and mashed kidney beans and cook until the tomatoes are soft. Season to taste with the Tabasco sauce.
4. Arrange half the corn chips in a flat ovenproof dish. Top with half the kidney bean mixture and then 125 g (4½ oz/1 cup) of the grated cheese.
5. Repeat with the remaining ingredients to make a second layer. Bake in the oven for 10–15 minutes, or until the cheese has melted and the nachos are heated through. Serve the nachos topped with guacamole (see page 21) and sour cream.

sticky chicken drumsticks

SERVES 4

- 2 tablespoons honey
- 2 tablespoons sweet chilli sauce
- 2 tablespoons tomato sauce (ketchup)
- 2 tablespoons dark soy sauce
- 2 tablespoons light soy sauce
- 1.5 kg (3 lb 5 oz) skinless chicken drumsticks
- 2 tablespoons sesame seeds

1. Put the honey, chilli sauce, tomato sauce and soy sauces in a large non-metallic dish and stir together. Cut 2–3 slits across each drumstick with a knife.
2. Coat the drumsticks in the marinade. Cover and refrigerate for at least 2 hours, or overnight. Turn in the marinade 2–3 times.
3. Preheat the oven to 180°C (350°F/Gas 4). Line a large baking tray with baking paper. Sprinkle the sesame seeds over the chicken and put them on the tray.
4. Bake for 45 minutes, or until cooked and golden, turning and brushing with the marinade 2–3 times. Serve warm or cold.

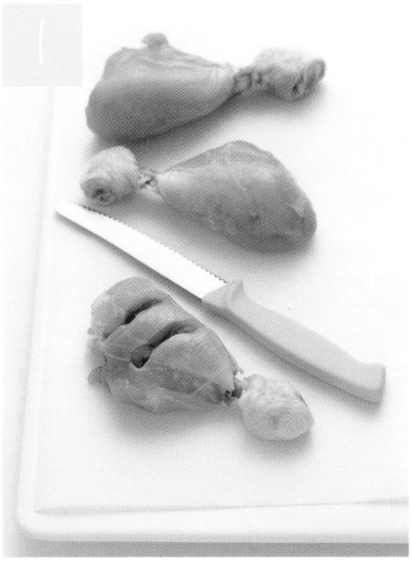

fresh spring rolls

MAKES 8

½ barbecued chicken

50 g (1¾ oz) dried mung bean vermicelli

8 x 17 cm (6½ inch) square dried rice paper wrappers

16 Thai basil leaves

1 large handful coriander (cilantro) leaves

1 carrot, cut into short thin strips and blanched

2 tablespoons plum sauce

1 Remove the meat from the chicken, discard the skin and finely shred the meat. Soak the vermicelli in hot water for 10 minutes and then drain.

2 Dip a rice paper wrapper into warm water for 10–15 seconds, or until it softens, then place it on a clean work surface. Put one-eighth of the chicken on the wrapper and top with two basil leaves, a few coriander leaves, a few carrot strips and a small amount of vermicelli. Spoon a little plum sauce over the top.

3 Press the filling down to flatten it a little, then fold in one side and roll it up tightly like a parcel. Lay the roll, seam side down, on a serving plate and sprinkle with a little water. Cover with a damp cloth and repeat with the remaining ingredients. Serve with your favourite dipping sauce or a little extra plum sauce.

cream of tomato soup

SERVES 4

1 tablespoon olive oil
1 onion, finely chopped
2 garlic cloves, crushed
1.25 kg (2 lb 12 oz) tinned crushed tomatoes
750 ml (26 fl oz/3 cups) chicken stock
1 tablespoon tomato paste (concentrated purée)
2 teaspoons soft brown sugar
250 ml (9 fl oz/1 cup) cream

1. Heat the oil in a large saucepan. Add the onion and cook until soft and lightly golden, stirring occasionally. Add the garlic and cook for 1 more minute.
2. Add the tomatoes, stock, tomato paste and sugar to the saucepan. Bring to the boil, then reduce the heat.
3. Simmer the soup, partially covered with a lid, for 20 minutes. Let the soup cool a little, then process in batches in a blender or food processor until smooth.
4. Return the soup to the pan, stir in the cream and reheat gently. Don't let the soup boil once you have added the cream, or it will curdle.

pumpkin soup

SERVES 4–6

1 kg (2 lb 4 oz) pumpkin (squash)
60 g (2¼ oz) butter
1 onion, chopped
1 litre (35 fl oz/4 cups) chicken stock
185 ml (6 fl oz/¾ cup) cream

1. Cut the pumpkin into large pieces, then cut off all the skin. Chop into smaller pieces. This is best done by an adult.
2. Heat the butter in a large saucepan. Add the onion and cook gently for 15 minutes, or until very soft.
3. Add the pumpkin and stock to the pan. Cover with a lid and bring to the boil, then reduce the heat and simmer for 20 minutes, or until the pumpkin is tender.
4. Let the soup cool a little, then process in batches in a blender or food processor until smooth.
5. Return the soup to the pan and add the cream and salt and pepper to taste. Stir over low heat until heated through. Don't let the soup boil once you have added the cream, or it will curdle.

chicken noodle omelette

SERVES 2

85 g (3 oz) packet chicken-flavoured instant noodles

175 g (6 oz/1 cup) chopped cooked chicken

2 teaspoons finely chopped flat-leaf (Italian) parsley

2 eggs, lightly beaten

2 tablespoons grated cheddar cheese

1. Boil 500 ml (17 fl oz/2 cups) of water in a saucepan. Add the noodles and flavour sachet to the saucepan. Cook the noodles as directed. Drain well.
2. Put the noodles, chicken, parsley and eggs in a bowl. Mix well.
3. Put the mixture in a 20 cm (8 inch) non-stick frying pan. Cook for 5 minutes without stirring.
4. Sprinkle with the cheese. Put under a hot grill (broiler) and grill (broil) for 2 minutes, or until browned. Serve hot.

corn fritters

SERVES 4

1 large red capsicum (pepper)

2–3 cobs fresh corn or 300 g (10½ oz/1½ cups) tinned corn kernels, drained

oil, for frying

2 tablespoons chopped flat-leaf (Italian) parsley, coriander (cilantro) leaves, chives or dill

3 eggs

1 Cut the capsicum into large pieces, discarding the seeds and membrane, then chop into small pieces. If using fresh corn, cut the kernels from the cob, using a sharp knife.

2 Heat 2 tablespoons of oil in a frying pan. Add the corn and capsicum and stir for 2 minutes. Transfer the vegetables to a bowl. Add the herbs and stir well to combine. Beat the eggs in a small bowl with a little pepper. Stir the egg gradually into the vegetable mixture.

3 Heat a non-stick frying pan over medium heat. Add enough oil to just cover the base. Drop large spoonfuls of the vegetable mixture into the pan, a few at a time. Cook the fritters for 1–2 minutes, or until brown. Turn and cook the other side. Drain on paper towels and keep warm while you cook the remainder.

strawberry shake

SERVES 2

175 g (6 oz/1 cup) chopped strawberries (or raspberries)

250 ml (9 fl oz/1 cup) milk

3 scoops vanilla or strawberry ice cream

sugar, to taste, if using raspberries

1. Put the strawberries or raspberries, milk and ice cream (and sugar, if using) into a blender and blend until smooth.
2. Pour into two cups and serve.

banana smoothie

SERVES 2

1 banana, roughly chopped

1 tablespoon plain yoghurt

1 teaspoon honey

250 ml (9 fl oz/1 cup) milk

1. Put the banana in a blender with the yoghurt, honey and milk and blend until smooth, thick and creamy.
2. Pour into two cups and serve.

berry froth

SERVES 2

220 g (7 3/4 oz/1 2/3 cup) fresh or frozen mixed berries

500 ml (17 fl oz/2 cups) milk

2 ice cubes

sugar, to taste

1. Put the mixed berries, milk and ice cubes in a blender and blend until smooth. Add the sugar and blend again until combined.
2. Pour into two large cups and serve.

fresh fruit slushy

SERVES 4

90 g (3 1/4 oz) fresh pineapple, peeled and cored, cut into chunks

1 banana, cut into chunks

3 kiwi fruit, sliced

250 ml (9 fl oz/1 cup) tropical fruit juice

2 ice cubes

1. Put the pineapple and banana in a blender with the kiwi fruit, fruit juice and ice cubes and blend until smooth.
2. Pour into four cups and serve.

malted milkshake

SERVES 2

250 ml (9 fl oz/1 cup) milk

1 tablespoon powdered drinking chocolate

1 tablespoon powdered malt

4 scoops vanilla ice cream

1. Combine the milk, drinking chocolate, malt and ice cream in a blender and blend for 1 minute.
2. Pour into two glasses and serve.

mango whiz

SERVES 1

70 g (2½ oz/½ cup) ice cubes

280 g (10 oz/1½ cups) chopped fresh mango

1. Put the ice cubes in a blender and blend until roughly chopped.
2. Add the mango and blend until the fruit and ice are well mixed.
3. Pour into a glass and serve. Add a little water or orange juice to make the drink a little thinner if you like.

peach dream

SERVES 4

425 g (15 oz) tinned peach slices, drained

500 ml (17 fl oz/2 cups) vanilla ice cream

3 tablespoons orange juice

2–3 drops vanilla extract

500 ml (17 fl oz/2 cups) chilled milk

1. Combine the peach slices, vanilla ice cream, orange juice, vanilla extract and chilled milk in a blender and blend until smooth.
2. Pour into four glasses and serve.

moo juice

SERVES 8

400 g (14 oz) fruit-flavoured yoghurt

2 tablespoons honey

1 teaspoon vanilla extract

2 ripe bananas

500 ml (17 fl oz/2 cups) chilled milk

4 scoops vanilla ice cream

1. Combine the yoghurt, honey, vanilla extract, bananas, milk and ice cream in a blender and blend for 3 minutes.
2. Divide among eight glasses and serve.

dinner time

pizza

SERVES 4

1 large fresh or frozen pizza base

tomato sauce

1 tablespoon olive oil

1 small onion, chopped

1 garlic clove, crushed

1 large tomato, chopped

1 tablespoon tomato paste (concentrated purée)

1/2 teaspoon dried oregano

napolitana topping

grated mozzarella cheese, chopped dried oregano, sliced pitted black olives and thinly sliced anchovy fillets (optional)

pepperoni topping

red capsicum (pepper), pepperoni and grated mozzarella cheese

1 To make the tomato sauce, heat the olive oil in a small saucepan over medium heat and add the onion and garlic. Cook for 3 minutes, or until soft.

2 Add the chopped tomato and stir to combine. Reduce the heat to low and simmer for 10 minutes, stirring occasionally.

3 Stir in the tomato paste and oregano and simmer for another 2 minutes. Set aside to cool.

4 Preheat the oven to 220°C (425°F/Gas 7). Put the pizza base on a non-stick pizza tray or a large baking tray lined with baking paper. Spread the tomato sauce over the pizza base.

5 Top with your favourite topping to make either a napolitana or pepperoni pizza. Bake for 30 minutes.

quick pasta with tomato sauce

SERVES 4

1 tablespoon extra virgin olive oil
1 garlic clove, crushed
400 g (14 oz) tinned chopped tomatoes
500 g (1 lb 2 oz) penne
1 tablespoon grated parmesan cheese

1. Heat the olive oil in a frying pan over medium heat. Cook the garlic, stirring constantly, for 30 seconds. Add the tomatoes and stir through. Reduce the heat to low and cook for a further 8–10 minutes, stirring occasionally, or until reduced.
2. Meanwhile, cook the pasta in a large saucepan of boiling water until just tender. Drain and return to the saucepan.
3. Add the cooked tomatoes to the pasta and stir through. Spoon into bowls and sprinkle with parmesan cheese.

fettucine carbonara

SERVES 4

2 teaspoons oil
8 bacon slices, cut into thin strips
500 g (1 lb 2 oz) fettucine
4 eggs
50 g (1 3/4 oz/1/2 cup) grated parmesan cheese
250 ml (9 fl oz/1 cup) cream

1. Heat the oil in a frying pan and cook the bacon over medium heat until brown and crisp. Remove from the pan and drain on paper towels.
2. Add the fettucine to a large saucepan of boiling water and cook until just tender. Drain well in a colander, then return to the pan.
3. Put the eggs, cheese and cream into a small bowl and beat together with a fork. Add the bacon.
4. Pour the sauce over the hot pasta. Stir over very low heat for 1 minute, or until the sauce thickens.

spaghetti bolognese

SERVES 4

- 1 teaspoon olive oil
- 1 large onion, finely chopped
- 3 garlic cloves, crushed
- 1 celery stalk, diced
- 1 carrot, diced
- 500 g (1 lb 2 oz) lean minced (ground) beef
- 1 tablespoon dried oregano
- 250 ml (9 fl oz/1 cup) red wine or water
- 500 ml (17 fl oz/2 cups) beef stock
- 2 tablespoons tomato paste (concentrated purée)
- 800 g (1 lb 12 oz) tinned chopped tomatoes
- 350 g (12 oz) spaghetti

1. Heat the oil in a non-stick saucepan over medium heat. Add the onion and cook for 2–3 minutes, or until softened. Add the garlic, celery and carrot and cook for 2–3 minutes, or until softened.
2. Add the beef and cook over high heat for 5 minutes, or until browned, breaking up any lumps with the back of a spoon.
3. Add the oregano and wine or water and cook for 3–4 minutes, or until almost all the liquid has evaporated. Add the stock, tomato paste and tomatoes and season with salt and pepper.
4. Reduce the heat to low and simmer, covered, for 1½ hours, stirring occasionally to prevent it from catching on the bottom. If the sauce is too thin, remove the lid and simmer until it has reduced and thickened.
5. Cook the pasta in a large saucepan of boiling water for 10 minutes, or until tender. Drain and toss through the bolognese sauce.

lasagne

SERVES 6

1 tablespoon olive oil
1 large onion, finely chopped
3 large garlic cloves, crushed
1 celery stalk, diced
1 carrot, diced
125 g (4½ oz) button mushrooms, sliced
500 g (1 lb 2 oz) lean minced (ground) beef
1 teaspoon dried oregano
250 ml (9 fl oz/1 cup) red wine or water
500 ml (17 fl oz/2 cups) beef stock
2 tablespoons tomato paste (concentrated purée)
800 g (1 lb 12 oz) tinned chopped tomatoes
500 g (1 lb 2 oz) English spinach
20 g (¾ oz) butter
4 tablespoons plain (all-purpose) flour
375 ml (13 fl oz/1½ cups) milk
150 g (5½ oz/⅔ cup) ricotta cheese
375 g (13 oz) fresh lasagne sheets
85 g (3 oz/⅔ cup) grated cheddar cheese

1 Heat the oil in a large pan over high heat. Add the onion and cook for 2 minutes. Add the garlic, celery, carrot and mushrooms and cook for 2 minutes. Add the beef and cook for 5 minutes, or until cooked. Add the oregano and cook for 3–4 minutes.

2 Add the wine, stock, tomato paste and tomatoes and season. Reduce the heat to low and simmer, covered, for 1½ hours, stirring occasionally. Cool slightly. Wilt the washed spinach for 1 minute in a covered pan.

3 To make the white sauce, melt the butter in a saucepan over medium heat. Stir in the flour and cook for 1 minute. Slowly stir in the milk, and keep stirring until the sauce boils and thickens. Simmer for 2 minutes. Stir in the ricotta until smooth.

4 Preheat the oven to 200°C (400°F/Gas 6). Arrange a third of the pasta over the base of a large ovenproof dish. Spread with half the beef, then half the spinach. Make another layer of pasta and spread with the remaining beef, then the spinach, then the remaining pasta. Top with the white sauce, sprinkle with cheddar and bake for 30 minutes, or until golden.

spaghetti with chicken meatballs

SERVES 4

tomato sauce

1 teaspoon olive oil

2 garlic cloves, crushed

800 g (1 lb 12 oz) tinned crushed tomatoes

chicken meatballs

500 g (1 lb 2 oz) minced (ground) chicken

2 garlic cloves, crushed

20 g (3/4 oz/1/4 cup) fresh breadcrumbs

2 tablespoons chopped basil

1/4 teaspoon cayenne pepper

1 tablespoon olive oil

2 tablespoons chopped basil

375 g (13 oz) spaghetti

30 g (1 oz) parmesan cheese, grated

1 To make the tomato sauce, heat the oil in a large non-stick saucepan over medium heat. Add the garlic and cook for 1 minute, or until just turning golden. Add the tomatoes and season. Reduce the heat and simmer for 15 minutes, or until thickened.

2 Line a baking tray with baking paper. To make the meatballs, combine the chicken, garlic, breadcrumbs, basil and cayenne pepper in a large bowl and season.

3 Using damp hands, roll tablespoons of the mixture into balls and place on the tray.

4 Heat the olive oil in a frying pan over medium heat. Cook the meatballs in batches, turning, for 3–4 minutes, or until golden. Transfer the meatballs to the sauce and simmer for a further 10 minutes, or until cooked through. Add the basil.

5 Meanwhile, cook the spaghetti in a large saucepan of boiling water for 10 minutes, or until tender. Drain well. Toss the spaghetti with the meatballs and sauce and serve with the grated parmesan.

san choy bau

SERVES 4

3 tablespoons oyster sauce

2 teaspoons soy sauce

3 tablespoons sherry

1 teaspoon sugar

1 1/2 tablespoons vegetable oil

1/4 teaspoon sesame oil

3 garlic cloves, crushed

3 teaspoons grated fresh ginger

6 spring onions (scallions), sliced on the diagonal

500 g (1 lb 2 oz) ground (minced) pork

100 g (3 1/2 oz) bamboo shoots, finely chopped

100 g (3 1/2 oz) water chestnuts, drained and finely chopped

1 tablespoon pine nuts, toasted

12 small or 4 large whole lettuce leaves (such as iceberg)

oyster sauce, to serve

1. To make the sauce, combine the oyster and soy sauces, sherry and sugar in a small bowl and stir until the sugar dissolves.
2. Heat a wok over high heat, add the vegetable and sesame oils and swirl to coat the wok. Add the garlic, ginger and half the spring onion and stir-fry for 1 minute. Add the pork and cook for 3–4 minutes, or until just cooked, breaking up any lumps.
3. Add the bamboo shoots, water chestnuts and remaining spring onion, then pour in the sauce. Cook for 2–3 minutes, or until the liquid thickens a little. Stir in the pine nuts.
4. Trim the lettuce leaves into cup shapes. Divide the filling among the lettuce cups to make either 12 small portions or four very large ones. Drizzle with oyster sauce, then serve.

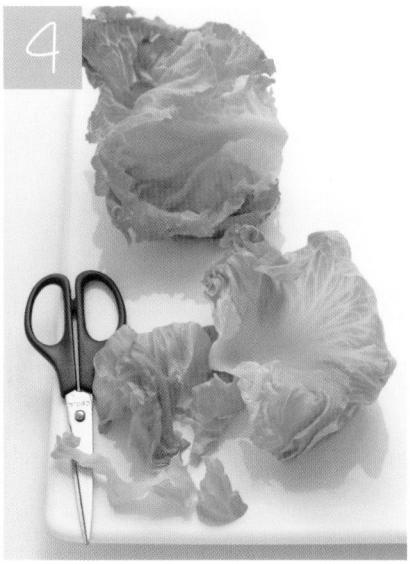

orange and ginger chicken stir-fry

SERVES 4–6

3 tablespoons vegetable oil

4–6 boneless, skinless chicken thighs, cut into small pieces

3 teaspoons grated fresh ginger

1 teaspoon grated orange zest

125 ml (4 fl oz/1/2 cup) chicken stock

2 teaspoons honey

550 g (1 lb 4 oz) bok choy (pak choy), trimmed and halved lengthways

toasted sesame seeds, to serve

steamed white rice, to serve

1 Heat a wok over high heat, add the oil and swirl to coat the side of the wok. Add the chicken in batches and stir-fry each batch for 3–4 minutes, or until golden.

2 Return all the chicken to the wok, add the ginger and orange zest and cook for 20 seconds, or until fragrant.

3 Add the stock and the honey and stir to combine. Increase the heat and cook for 3–4 minutes, or until the sauce has thickened slightly.

4 Add the bok choy and cook until slightly wilted. Season well, then sprinkle with toasted sesame seeds and serve with steamed rice.

sweet chilli chicken and noodles

SERVES 4

375 g (13 oz) hokkien (egg) noodles

4 boneless, skinless chicken thighs, cut into small pieces

1–2 tablespoons sweet chilli sauce

2 teaspoons fish sauce

1 tablespoon vegetable oil

100 g (3½ oz) baby sweet corn, halved lengthways

150 g (5½ oz) snow peas (mangetout), topped and tailed

1 tablespoon lime juice

1. Put the noodles in a large bowl, cover with boiling water for 1 minute, then gently separate. Drain and rinse.
2. Combine the chicken, sweet chilli sauce and fish sauce in a bowl.
3. Heat a wok over high heat, add the oil and swirl to coat the side of the wok. Add the chicken and stir-fry for 3–5 minutes, or until cooked through. Add the corn and snow peas and stir-fry for 2 minutes. Stir in the noodles and lime juice, then serve.

pork, pumpkin and cashew stir-fry

SERVES 4

- 2–3 tablespoons vegetable oil
- 80 g (2 3/4 oz/1/2 cup) cashews
- 750 g (1 lb 10 oz) pork loin fillet
- 500 g (1 lb 2 oz) pumpkin (squash), cut into cubes
- 1 tablespoon grated fresh ginger
- 4 tablespoons chicken stock
- 3 tablespoons dry sherry
- 1 1/2 tablespoons soy sauce
- 1/2 teaspoon cornflour (cornstarch)
- 300 g (10 1/2 oz) bok choy (pak choy)
- 1–2 tablespoons coriander (cilantro) leaves

1. Heat a wok over high heat, add 1 tablespoon of the oil and swirl to coat the wok. Stir-fry the cashews for 1–2 minutes, or until browned. Remove and drain on paper towel.
2. Slice the pork thinly across the grain. Reheat the wok, add a little extra oil and swirl to coat. Stir-fry the pork in batches for 5 minutes, or until lightly browned. Remove. Add 1 tablespoon of oil and stir-fry the pumpkin and ginger for 3 minutes, or until lightly browned. Add the stock, sherry and soy sauce, and simmer for 3 minutes, or until the pumpkin is tender.
3. Blend the cornflour with 1 teaspoon of water, add to the wok and stir until the mixture boils and thickens. Return the pork and cashews to the wok, and add the bok choy and coriander. Stir until the bok choy has just wilted. Serve with steamed rice.

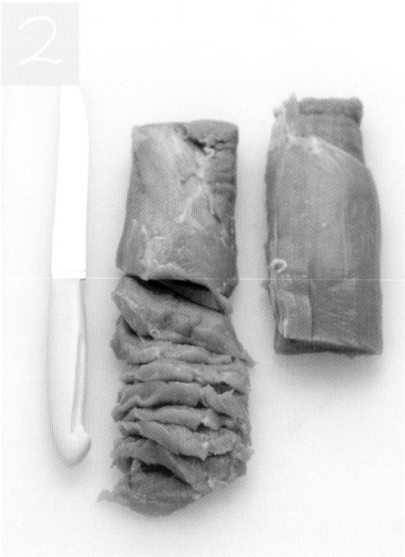

spinach and ricotta cannelloni

SERVES 4

20 g (3/4 oz) unsalted butter
1 small onion, finely chopped
2 garlic cloves, crushed
3 bunches English spinach
300 g (10 1/2 oz/1 1/4 cups) ricotta cheese
1 tablespoon dried oregano

tomato sauce

1 tablespoon olive oil
1 small onion, finely chopped
2 garlic cloves, crushed
440 g (15 1/2 oz) tinned tomatoes
125 ml (4 fl oz/1/2 cup) tomato pasta sauce
1 teaspoon dried oregano
2 teaspoons dijon mustard
1 tablespoon balsamic vinegar
1 teaspoon sugar

375 g (13 oz) fresh lasagne sheets
70 g (2 1/2 oz) grated mozzarella cheese
50 g (1 3/4 oz) grated parmesan cheese

1 Preheat the oven to 180°C (350°F/Gas 4). To make the filling, melt the butter in a saucepan and cook the onion and garlic for 3–5 minutes until softened. Shred the spinach, add to the pan and cook for 5 minutes, or until wilted and the moisture has evaporated. Remove from the heat and leave to cool. Put in a blender with the ricotta and oregano and process until smooth.

2 To make the sauce, heat the oil in a saucepan and cook the onion and garlic over low heat for 5 minutes. Add the rest of the sauce ingredients. Bring to the boil, then simmer for 10 minutes, or until thick.

3 Cut the lasagne sheets into twelve 12 cm (4 1/2 inch) squares. Lightly grease a large ovenproof dish and spread a third of the sauce over the base.

4 Spoon spinach filling down the side of each lasagne square, then roll up the pasta around the filling and put, seam side down, in the dish. Space out the cannelloni evenly, then spread the remaining sauce over the top. Sprinkle with grated mozzarella and parmesan and bake for 30–35 minutes, or until golden.

pea and ham risotto

SERVES 4

1 tablespoon olive oil

1 celery stalk, chopped

2 tablespoons chopped flat-leaf (Italian) parsley

70 g (2½ oz) sliced ham, chopped

250 g (9 oz/1⅔ cups) peas (fresh or frozen)

750 ml (26 fl oz/3 cups) chicken stock

60 g (2¼ oz) unsalted butter

1 onion, chopped

440 g (15½ oz/2 cups) risotto rice

35 g (1¼ oz/⅓ cup) grated parmesan cheese, plus extra to serve

1. Heat the oil in a frying pan and add the celery and parsley. Cook over medium heat for a few minutes. Add the ham and stir for 1 minute. Add the peas and 3 tablespoons of water and bring to the boil, then reduce the heat and simmer, uncovered, until almost all the liquid has evaporated. Set aside. Put the stock and 750 ml (26 fl oz/3 cups) of water in a saucepan and keep at simmering point.
2. Heat the butter in a saucepan. Add the onion and stir until softened. Add the rice and stir well. Pour in 3 tablespoons of water. Add 125 ml (4 fl oz/½ cup) of stock to the rice mixture. Stir over low heat until the stock has been absorbed. Repeat until all the stock has been added and the rice is creamy and tender.
3. Add the pea mixture and parmesan and serve with the extra parmesan.

chicken and leek risotto

SERVES 4–6

60 g (2¼ oz) unsalted butter

1 leek, thinly sliced

2 boneless, skinless chicken breasts, finely chopped

440 g (15½ oz/2 cups) risotto rice

1.25 litres (44 fl oz/5 cups) chicken stock

35 g (1¼ oz/⅓ cup) grated parmesan cheese

1. Preheat the oven to 150°C (300°F/Gas 2). Heat the butter in an ovenproof dish with a lid over medium heat. Add the leek and cook for 2 minutes, or until softened but not browned.
2. Add the chicken and cook, stirring, for 2–3 minutes, or until it is golden on both sides. Add the rice and stir so that it is well coated with butter. Cook for 1 minute.
3. Add the stock and 3 tablespoons of water and bring to the boil. Cover and bake in the oven for 30 minutes, stirring halfway through cooking time. Remove from the oven and stir through the parmesan. Season.

pork and chive dumplings

MAKES 24

1 teaspoon vegetable oil
2 garlic cloves, crushed
1 teaspoon finely grated fresh ginger
2 teaspoons snipped chives
1/2 carrot, finely diced
200 g (7 oz) minced (ground) pork
2 tablespoons oyster sauce
3 teaspoons salt-reduced soy sauce, plus extra to serve
1/2 teaspoon sesame oil
1 teaspoon cornflour (cornstarch)
24 round gow gee wrappers

1. Heat a wok over high heat, add the vegetable oil and swirl to coat the side of the wok. Add the garlic, ginger, chives and carrot, then stir-fry for 2 minutes. Remove the wok from the heat.
2. Put the pork, oyster sauce, soy sauce, sesame oil and cornflour in a bowl and mix well. Add the vegetable mixture once it has cooled, mixing it into the pork mixture.
3. Put 2 teaspoons of the mixture in the centre of each gow gee wrapper. Moisten the edges with water, then fold in half to form a semicircle. Pinch the edges together to form a ruffled edge.
4. Line a double bamboo steamer with baking paper. Put half the dumplings in a single layer in each steamer basket. Cover and steam over a wok of simmering water for 12 minutes, or until cooked through. Serve with soy sauce.

sausage pie

SERVES 4

3 thick or 6 thin sausages

4 sheets frozen puff pastry, thawed

4 eggs

1 Put the sausages in a large bowl and cover with boiling water. Leave until cool. When cool, carefully peel the skins from the sausages and slice.

2 Use half the pastry to line a 25 cm (10 inch) pie dish or four individual dishes. Arrange the sausages evenly in the dish. Beat the eggs and season with salt and pepper, then gently pour over the sausages.

3 Preheat the oven to 190°C (375°F/Gas 5). Use the rest of the pastry to make a lid for the pie, trim the excess and seal the edges well. Cut two small slits in the middle. Cut out star shapes and place on top, if desired. Brush with some beaten egg.

4 Bake for 45 minutes. Serve hot or cold.

burger with the works

SERVES 4

burgers

500 g (1 lb 2 oz) lean minced (ground) beef

1 onion, finely chopped

1 egg, lightly beaten

25 g (1 oz/1/3 cup) fresh breadcrumbs

2 tablespoons tomato sauce (ketchup)

2 teaspoons Worcestershire sauce

toppings

30 g (1 oz) butter

2 large onions, cut into rings

4 cheddar cheese slices

4 bacon slices

4 eggs

4 large hamburger buns, halved

1 handful lettuce leaves

1 large tomato, sliced

4 pineapple rings

tomato sauce (ketchup), to serve

1. Place all the burger ingredients in a mixing bowl. Use your hands to mix together until well combined.
2. Divide the mixture into 4 portions and shape each portion into a patty.
3. Melt the butter in a frying pan and cook the onion until soft. Set aside and keep warm.
4. Cook the burgers in the frying pan for 4 minutes each side. Place a slice of cheese on each burger, to melt.
5. Cook the bacon in the frying pan (without any butter) until crisp, then fry the eggs.
6. Toast the buns under a hot grill (broiler) for 3–5 minutes and place the bases on serving plates. On each base, place the lettuce, tomato and pineapple, then a burger. Follow with bacon, onion, egg, tomato sauce and finally the bun top.

fried rice

SERVES 4

2 tablespoons peanut oil

2 eggs, well beaten

4 bacon slices, chopped

2 teaspoons finely grated fresh ginger

1 garlic clove, crushed

6 spring onions (scallions), finely chopped

50 g (1 3/4 oz) red capsicum (pepper), seeded and diced

1 teaspoon sesame oil

750 g (1 lb 10 oz/4 cups) cold, cooked long-grain white rice

100 g (3 1/2 oz/2/3 cup) frozen peas, thawed

100 g (3 1/2 oz) cooked chicken, chopped

2 tablespoons soy sauce

1. Heat a large heavy-based wok until very hot. Add about 2 teaspoons of the peanut oil and swirl to coat the wok. Pour in the eggs and swirl to coat a little up the side of the wok. Cook until just set into an omelette. Remove from the wok, roll up and set aside.
2. Add the remaining peanut oil to the wok and stir-fry the bacon for 2 minutes. Add the ginger, garlic, spring onion and capsicum and stir-fry for 2 minutes.
3. Add the sesame oil and the rice. Stir-fry, tossing regularly, until the rice is heated through.
4. Cut the omelette into thin strips and add to the wok with the peas and the chicken. Cover and steam for 1 minute, or until heated through. Stir in the soy sauce and serve.

potato gnocchi with tomato sauce

SERVES 4–6

tomato sauce

1 tablespoon oil

1 onion, chopped

1 celery stalk, chopped

2 carrots, chopped

850 g (1 lb 14 oz) tinned crushed tomatoes

1 teaspoon sugar

potato gnocchi

1 kg (2 lb 4 oz) all-purpose potatoes

30 g (1 oz) butter

250 g (9 oz/2 cups) plain (all purpose) flour

2 eggs, beaten

1 To make the tomato sauce, heat the oil in a saucepan, add the onion, celery and carrot and cook for about 5 minutes, stirring. Add the tomatoes and sugar and season. Bring to the boil, then reduce the heat to very low and simmer for 20 minutes. Cool a little, then process, in batches, in a food processor until smooth.

2 To make the potato gnocchi, peel the potatoes, chop roughly and boil until very tender. Drain and mash until smooth. Using a wooden spoon, stir in the butter and flour, then beat in the eggs. Leave to cool.

3 Turn the gnocchi mixture out onto a floured surface and divide into four. Roll each into a sausage shape.

4 Cut into short pieces and press each piece with the back of a fork. Cook the gnocchi in batches in a large saucepan of boiling salted water for about 2 minutes, or until they rise to the surface. Using a slotted spoon, drain the gnocchi and transfer to bowls. Serve with the tomato sauce.

beer-battered fish and wedges

SERVES 4

3 all-purpose potatoes

oil, for deep-frying

125 g (4½ oz/1 cup) self-raising flour

1 egg, beaten

185 ml (6 fl oz/¾ cup) beer

4 boneless white fish fillets

plain (all-purpose) flour, for dusting

125 g (4½ oz/½ cup) tartare sauce, or mayonnaise mixed with 1 tablespoon lemon juice

1 Wash the potatoes, but do not peel. Cut into thick wedges, then dry with paper towels. Fill a heavy-based saucepan two-thirds full with oil and heat. Gently lower the potato wedges into medium–hot oil. Cook for 4 minutes, or until tender and lightly browned. Carefully remove the wedges from the oil with a slotted spoon and drain on paper towels.

2 Sift the self-raising flour with some pepper into a large bowl and make a well in the centre. Add the egg and beer. Using a wooden spoon, stir until just combined and smooth. Dust the fish fillets in the plain flour, shaking off the excess. Add the fish fillets one at a time to the batter and toss until well coated. Remove the fish from the batter, draining off the excess batter.

3 Working with one piece of fish at a time, gently lower it into the medium–hot oil. Cook for 2 minutes, or until golden and crisp and cooked through. Carefully remove from the oil with a slotted spoon. Drain on paper towels, and keep warm while you cook the remainder.

4 Return the potato wedges to the medium–hot oil. Cook for another 2 minutes, or until golden brown and crisp. Remove from the oil with a slotted spoon and drain on paper towels. Serve the wedges immediately with the fish, and tartare sauce or lemon mayonnaise.

Note: This recipe has ingredients that are deep-fried, so you'll need an adult to help you if you are cooking on your own.

fishcakes

SERVES 4

700 g (1 lb 9 oz) all-purpose potatoes, peeled and quartered

2 tablespoons canola oil

500 g (1 lb 2 oz) boneless white fish fillets

1 leek, white part only, finely chopped

2 garlic cloves, crushed

30 g (1 oz) chopped spring onions (scallions)

lemon wedges, to serve

1. Put the potato in a saucepan. Cover with cold water and bring to the boil. Boil for 15 minutes, or until the potato is tender. Drain well. Mash with a fork.
2. Meanwhile, heat 2 teaspoons of the oil in a large non-stick frying pan over medium heat. Add the fish fillets and cook for 3–4 minutes on each side, or until cooked. Set aside to cool. Flake the fish with a fork.
3. Heat another 2 teaspoons of the oil in the same frying pan over medium heat. Cook the leek and garlic, stirring often, for 5–6 minutes, or until the leek softens. Set aside on a plate.
4. Mix together the mashed potato, flaked fish, leek mixture and spring onion in a large bowl. Shape into eight cakes and put on a plate. Cover and refrigerate for 1 hour.
5. Heat the remaining oil in the frying pan over medium heat. Cook the fish cakes for 3–4 minutes on each side, or until lightly golden.

tuna enchiladas

MAKES 8

1 tablespoon light olive oil
1 onion, thinly sliced
3 garlic cloves, crushed
2 teaspoons ground cumin
125 ml (4 fl oz/1/2 cup) vegetable stock
425 g (15 oz) tinned tuna in brine, drained
3 tomatoes, peeled, deseeded and chopped
1 tablespoon tomato paste (concentrated purée)
425 g (15 oz) tinned three-bean mix
2 tablespoons chopped coriander (cilantro) leaves
8 flour tortillas
1 small avocado, chopped
125 g (4 1/2 oz/1/2 cup) light sour cream
1 handful coriander (cilantro) sprigs
115 g (4 oz/2 cups) shredded lettuce

1. Preheat the oven to 170°C (325°F/Gas 3). Heat the oil in a deep frying pan over medium heat. Add the onion and cook for 3–4 minutes, or until just soft. Add the garlic and cook for another 30 seconds. Add the cumin, vegetable stock, tuna, tomato and tomato paste and cook for 6–8 minutes, or until the mixture is thick.
2. Drain and rinse the bean mix. Add the beans to the sauce and cook for 5 minutes to heat through, then add the chopped coriander.
3. Meanwhile, wrap the tortillas in foil and warm in the oven for 3–4 minutes.
4. Place a tortilla on a plate and spread with a large scoop of the bean mixture. Top with some avocado, sour cream, coriander sprigs and lettuce. Roll the enchiladas up, tucking in the ends.

vegetarian chilli

SERVES 6

130 g (4½ oz/¾ cup) burghul (bulgur)

2 tablespoons olive oil

1 onion, finely chopped

2 garlic cloves, crushed

2 teaspoons ground cumin

1 teaspoon chilli powder

½ teaspoon ground cinnamon

820 g (1 lb 13 oz) tinned crushed tomatoes

750 ml (26 fl oz/3 cups) vegetable stock

440 g (15½ oz) tinned red kidney beans, rinsed and drained

440 g (15½ oz) tinned chickpeas, rinsed and drained

315 g (11 oz) tinned corn kernels, rinsed and drained

2 tablespoons tomato paste (concentrated purée)

plain yoghurt, to serve

1 Put the burghul in a heatproof bowl and pour in 250 ml (9 fl oz/1 cup) of hot water. Leave to stand until needed.

2 Heat the oil in a large saucepan and add the onion. Cook for about 10 minutes over medium heat, stirring occasionally, or until soft and lightly golden. Add the garlic, cumin, chilli and cinnamon and stir-fry for 1 minute.

3 Add the burghul and all the remaining ingredients, except the yoghurt, and stir to combine. Reduce the heat to low and simmer for 30 minutes. Serve with a dollop of yoghurt.

bubble and squeak

SERVES 4–6

150 g (5½ oz) potato, cooked
150 g (5½ oz) pumpkin (squash), cooked
50 g (1¾ oz/1 cup) grated cabbage, cooked
50 g (1¾ oz) small broccoli florets, cooked
4 eggs, beaten
2 chives, snipped
20 g (¾ oz) unsalted butter

1. Put the vegetables in a bowl and mix well with the egg and chives.
2. Melt the butter in a large frying pan and add the vegetable mixture. Cook over medium heat until the underside is golden, then cut into quarters and turn over. Cook the mixture for a little longer, until it is golden and the egg has set.

tofu with greens and noodles

SERVES 4

marinade

3 tablespoons oyster sauce

3 tablespoons hoisin sauce

2 tablespoons soy sauce

1 1/2 tablespoons soft brown sugar

3 teaspoons grated fresh ginger

3 garlic cloves, crushed

300 g (10 1/2 oz) firm tofu, drained and cut into small cubes

300 g (10 1/2 oz) dried thin egg noodles

1 teaspoon canola oil

4 red Asian shallots, thinly sliced

1 small red capsicum (pepper), seeded and thinly sliced

200 g (7 oz) sugar snap peas, trimmed

400 g (14 oz) broccoli, cut into 5 cm (2 inch) lengths

125 ml (4 fl oz/1/2 cup) vegetable stock or water

1 Combine the marinade ingredients in a non-metallic bowl. Add the tofu and gently stir through. Cover and refrigerate for at least 30 minutes.

2 Cook the noodles according to the directions and drain. Cut the noodles into short lengths with scissors.

3 Heat the oil in a large wok. Add the shallots and capsicum and stir-fry for 2 minutes, or until slightly softened. Add the peas, broccoli and stock. Cover and cook for 2–3 minutes, or until the vegetables are just tender, stirring occasionally.

4 Add the tofu with the marinade and the noodles. Gently combine and stir until heated through. Serve immediately.

leek and cheese frittata

SERVES 6

2 tablespoons olive oil
3 leeks, white part only, thinly sliced
2 zucchini (courgettes), thinly sliced
1 garlic clove, crushed
5 eggs, lightly beaten
4 tablespoons grated parmesan cheese
4 tablespoons diced Swiss cheese

1. Heat 1 tablespoon of the olive oil in a small frying pan. Add the leek and cook, stirring, over low heat until slightly softened. Cover and cook the leek for 10 minutes, stirring occasionally. Add the zucchini and garlic and cook for another 10 minutes. Transfer the mixture to a bowl. Allow to cool, then season with pepper. Add the egg and cheeses and stir through.
2. Heat the remaining oil in the pan, then add the egg mixture and smooth the surface. Cook over low heat for 15 minutes, or until the frittata is almost set.
3. Put the pan under a hot grill (broiler) for 3–5 minutes, or until the top is set and golden. Allow the frittata to stand for 5 minutes before cutting into wedges and serving. Serve with a fresh green salad.

eat your greens

asparagus with parmesan

SERVES 2–4

155 g (5½ oz) asparagus spears

olive oil, for drizzling

grated parmesan cheese, to serve

1 Gently bend the base of each asparagus spear to snap off the woody end.

2 Put the asparagus in a large frying pan and pour in enough hot water to just cover them. Put a lid on the pan and cook the asparagus for 2 minutes, or until they are bright green and crisply tender. Drain well.

3 Serve drizzled with a little olive oil and sprinkled with freshly grated parmesan cheese.

caesar salad

SERVES 4

4 slices white bread or sourdough, crusts removed and cut into cubes

3 bacon slices

2 baby cos or 1 cos lettuce

50 g (1 3/4 oz) parmesan cheese shavings

dressing

4 anchovies, chopped

1 egg yolk

2 tablespoons lemon juice

1 garlic clove, crushed

125 ml (4 fl oz/1/2 cup) olive oil

1. Preheat the oven to 190°C (375°F/Gas 5). Spread the bread cubes on a baking tray and bake for 10 minutes, or until golden.
2. Fry the bacon slices in a frying pan over medium heat until crisp. Drain on paper towels. Put the lettuce leaves in a salad bowl with the bread cubes, bacon and parmesan.
3. To make the dressing, put the anchovies, egg yolk, lemon, juice and garlic in a blender. Blend for 20 seconds, or until smooth. Add the oil in a thin, steady stream until the dressing is creamy. Drizzle over the salad.

greek salad

SERVES 4

1 green capsicum (pepper)

150 g (5½ oz) feta cheese

2 large or 3 small vine-ripened tomatoes, cut into wedges

1 Lebanese (short) cucumber, sliced

1 small red onion, thinly sliced (optional)

60 g (2¼ oz/⅓ cup) kalamata olives

2–3 tablespoons lemon juice

3–4 tablespoons olive oil

1. Cut the capsicum in half lengthways and remove the white seeds and membrane. Cut the flesh into small squares.
2. Cut the feta cheese into small cubes.
3. Combine the capsicum, cheese, tomato, cucumber, onion and olives in a large bowl. Drizzle with the lemon juice and oil. Sprinkle with salt and pepper. Toss gently to combine, then serve.

mixed salad

SERVES 4

1 oak leaf lettuce

100 g (3½ oz) baby rocket (arugula)

1 small red capsicum (pepper)

250 g (9 oz) cherry tomatoes, cut into wedges

1 Lebanese (short) cucumber, thinly sliced

2–3 tablespoons snipped chives

vinaigrette

3 tablespoons olive oil

2–3 tablespoons white vinegar or lemon juice

1 teaspoon sugar

1. Tear the lettuce and rocket leaves into pieces and put in a large serving bowl.
2. Cut the capsicum in half lengthways and remove the seeds and white membrane. Cut into thin strips.
3. Combine the capsicum, tomato, cucumber and chives in the bowl with the lettuce and rocket.
4. To make the vinaigrette, whisk the oil, vinegar and sugar in a small bowl. Season with some salt and pepper. Pour the vinaigrette over the salad just before serving.

hash browns

SERVES 4

2 all-purpose potatoes

oil, for frying

1. Fill a saucepan with water and bring to the boil. Peel the potatoes and cut them in half.
2. Put the potatoes into the saucepan. Bring the water back to the boil, then boil for 10 minutes, or until just tender when pierced with a knife.
3. Drain the potatoes and leave until cool enough to handle. Grate the potatoes, put in a bowl and season with salt and pepper. Mix through.
4. Shape the grated potato roughly into patties about 10 cm (4 inches) round.
5. Heat enough oil to cover the bottom of the frying pan and cook the patties for a few minutes on each side, or until golden brown and crispy. Drain on paper towels.

ratatouille

SERVES 6

2 tablespoons olive oil
1 large onion, chopped
2 garlic cloves, crushed
3 slender eggplants (aubergines)
3 small zucchini (courgettes)
1 green capsicum (pepper)
1 red capsicum (pepper)
3 large tomatoes, chopped
1 large handful basil, chopped

1. Heat the oil in a large saucepan and add the onion. Cook over medium heat for 10 minutes, or until brown. Add the garlic and cook for 1 more minute.
2. Meanwhile, slice the eggplants and zucchini fairly thickly.
3. Remove the seeds and white membranes from the capsicums and cut into small squares.
4. Add all the vegetables to the pan. Cook, stirring frequently, for about 5 minutes. Reduce the heat to low, cover the pan with a lid and cook for 15 minutes, stirring occasionally. Uncover the pan, increase the heat and cook for another 5 minutes. Stir in the basil.

potato salad

SERVES 4

600 g (1 lb 5 oz) all-purpose potatoes

1/2 small red onion, finely chopped

2–3 celery stalks, finely chopped

1 small green capsicum (pepper), chopped

2 tablespoons finely chopped flat-leaf (Italian) parsley

dressing

185 g (6 1/2 oz/3/4 cup) mayonnaise

1–2 tablespoons white vinegar or lemon juice

2 tablespoons sour cream

1. Wash and peel the potatoes. Cut into small pieces. Cook the potato in a large saucepan of boiling water for about 5 minutes, or until just tender. Drain the potato and allow it to cool.
2. Combine the onion, celery, capsicum and parsley in a large bowl. Add the cooled potato.
3. To make the dressing, mix together the mayonnaise, vinegar or juice and sour cream. Season with salt and pepper.
4. Pour the dressing over the potato and gently toss to combine.

scalloped potatoes

SERVES 4

500 g (1 lb 2 oz) all-purpose potatoes

170 ml (5 1/2 fl oz/2/3 cup) milk

125 ml (4 fl oz/1/2 cup) cream

60 g (2 1/4 oz/1/2 cup) grated cheddar cheese

20 g (3/4 oz) butter

1. Preheat the oven to 180°C (350°F/Gas 4). Brush a 20 cm (8 inch) shallow ovenproof dish with melted butter or oil.
2. Peel the potatoes and cut into thin slices. Layer the slices in the dish, overlapping them slightly.
3. Combine the milk and the cream and drizzle over the potato.
4. Sprinkle the cheese evenly over the potato, then dot with the butter. Bake for 45 minutes, or until the potato is tender and the top is golden brown.

stir-fried chinese vegetables

SERVES 4

300 g (10½ oz) baby bok choy (pak choy)
100 g (3½ oz) snake (yard-long) beans
2 spring onions (scallions)
150 g (5½ oz) broccoli
1 red capsicum (pepper)
2 tablespoons oil
2 garlic cloves, crushed
2 teaspoons grated fresh ginger
1 tablespoon sesame oil
2 teaspoons soy sauce

1. Wash the bok choy and trim away the thick stalks. Cut the leaves into wide strips.
2. Cut the snake beans into 5 cm (2 inch) lengths and slice the spring onions diagonally. Cut the broccoli into small florets and the capsicum into strips.
3. Heat the oil in a large frying pan or wok. Add the garlic and ginger and cook over medium heat for 30 seconds, stirring constantly.
4. Add the beans, spring onion and broccoli and stir-fry for 3 minutes. Add the capsicum and stir-fry for 2 more minutes, then add the bok choy and stir for 1 more minute. Stir in the sesame oil and soy sauce and toss through. Serve immediately.

honey carrots

SERVES 4

2 carrots
30 g (1 oz) butter
1 tablespoon honey

1. Peel the carrots and cut into thin slices. Steam or boil the carrot for about 3 minutes, or until tender. Drain well and return to the pan.
2. Add the butter and honey and toss over medium heat until the butter has melted and the carrot is coated.

cauliflower cheese

SERVES 4

500 g (1 lb 2 oz) cauliflower, cut into florets
30 g (1 oz) butter
3 teaspoons plain (all-purpose) flour
185 ml (6 fl oz/3/4 cup) milk
60 g (2 1/4 oz/1/2 cup) grated cheddar cheese
25 g (1 oz/1/3 cup) fresh breadcrumbs

1. Steam or microwave the cauliflower for a few minutes until just tender. Arrange the cooked cauliflower in a shallow ovenproof dish.
2. Melt the butter in a small saucepan. Add the flour and cook, stirring, for 1 minute, or until golden.
3. Add the milk a little at a time, stirring until completely smooth between each addition.
4. When all the milk has been added, keep stirring over medium heat until the sauce boils and thickens. Simmer for 1 minute, still stirring.
5. Remove the pan from the heat and add almost all the cheese, reserving a couple of tablespoons. Stir until the cheese has melted.
6. Pour the sauce over the cauliflower. Sprinkle with the remaining cheese combined with the breadcrumbs.
7. Place under a hot grill (broiler) for a few minutes, until the cheese on top has melted and the breadcrumbs are golden brown.

stuffed capsicums

SERVES 4

4 small red capsicums (peppers)

110 g (3¾ oz/½ cup) short-grain white rice

1 tablespoon olive oil

1 onion, finely chopped

2 garlic cloves, crushed

1 tomato, chopped

125 g (4½ oz/1 cup) finely grated cheddar cheese

25 g (1 oz/¼ cup) finely grated parmesan cheese

1 handful basil, chopped

1 handful flat-leaf (Italian) parsley, chopped

1. Preheat the oven to 180°C (350°F/Gas 4). Cut the tops off the capsicums and scoop out the seeds and white membranes.
2. Cook the rice in a large saucepan of boiling water until tender. Drain well and set aside to cool.
3. Heat the oil in a frying pan and cook the onion for a few minutes until lightly golden. Add the garlic and cook for 1 more minute.
4. Add the onion and garlic to the rice, along with all the remaining ingredients. Mix everything together well and season with salt and pepper.
5. Spoon the rice filling into the capsicums and place on a baking tray. Bake for 30 minutes, or until the capsicums are soft and the filling is brown on top.

stuffed mushrooms

SERVES 4–6

8 large flat or 12 button mushrooms

2 tablespoons oil

1 small onion, finely chopped

4 bacon slices, chopped

80 g (2¾ oz/1 cup) fresh breadcrumbs

1 tablespoon chopped flat-leaf (Italian) parsley

65 g (2¼ oz/⅔ cup) grated parmesan cheese

1. Preheat the oven to 180°C (350°F/Gas 4). Brush a baking tray with melted butter or oil.
2. Remove the stems of the mushrooms. Finely chop the stems.
3. Heat the oil in a frying pan, add the onion and bacon and cook until the bacon is lightly browned. Add the chopped mushroom stems and cook for 1 minute.
4. Transfer the mixture to a bowl. Add the breadcrumbs, parsley and parmesan and stir to combine.
5. Place the mushroom caps onto the baking tray and spoon the filling into the caps. Bake for 20 minutes, or until the mushrooms are tender and the topping is golden. Serve immediately.

sticky puddings

pear and raspberry crumble

SERVES 6

6 large pears

2 tablespoons caster (superfine) sugar

3 star anise

125 g (4½ oz/1 cup) raspberries

125 g (4½ oz/1 cup) plain (all-purpose) flour

95 g (3¼ oz/½ cup) soft brown sugar

100 g (3½ oz) unsalted butter, cut into cubes

ice cream, to serve

1 Preheat the oven to 190°C (375°F/Gas 5). Peel, quarter and core the pears, then cut each piece in half lengthways. Put into a large saucepan and sprinkle with the sugar. Add 1 tablespoon of water and the star anise. Cover and bring to the boil.

2 Cook, covered, over medium–low heat for 10 minutes, stirring occasionally, until the fruit is tender but still holds its shape. Drain the pears and discard the star anise. Transfer to a large ovenproof dish or six 250 ml (9 fl oz/1 cup) ramekins. Sprinkle the raspberries over the pears.

3 Combine the flour, sugar and butter in a bowl. Use your fingertips to rub the butter into the flour, until the mixture resembles coarse breadcrumbs. Sprinkle over the fruit, then bake for 20–25 minutes, until golden brown. Leave for 5 minutes, then serve with ice cream.

pavlova

SERVES 6–8

4 egg whites

1/2 teaspoon cream of tartar

230 g (8 oz/1 cup) caster (superfine) sugar

2 tablespoons icing (confectioners') sugar

375 ml (13 fl oz/1 1/2 cups) cream

banana, raspberries and blueberries, to serve

pulp from 2 passionfruit, to decorate

1 Preheat the oven to 150°C (300°F/Gas 2). Line a baking tray with baking paper. Draw a 20 cm (8 inch) circle on the paper.

2 Using electric beaters, beat the egg whites in a large, dry bowl until soft peaks form. Add the cream of tartar. Gradually add the caster sugar, beating well after each addition. Continue beating until the mixture is thick and glossy and the sugar has completely dissolved. Add the icing sugar and beat.

3 To test if the sugar has dissolved, rub a small amount of the mixture between your thumb and forefinger. The mixture should feel just slightly gritty. If it feels very gritty, continue beating for a few more minutes.

4 Spread the meringue mixture onto the tray, inside the marked circle. Bake for 40 minutes.

5 Whip the cream until soft peaks form. Slice the banana. Decorate the pavlova with cream and the fresh fruit. Spoon the passionfruit pulp over the top and serve immediately.

baked apples

SERVES 4

4 cooking apples
80 g (2 3/4 oz/1/3 cup) soft brown sugar
1 1/2 tablespoons chopped raisins
1/2 teaspoon ground cinnamon (optional)
20 g (3/4 oz) unsalted butter
yoghurt or cream, to serve

1. Preheat the oven to 220°C (425°F/Gas 7). Core the apples and score the skin around the middle.
2. Combine the sugar, raisins and cinnamon, if using, in a bowl.
3. Place each apple on a piece of foil and stuff it with the filling. Spread a little butter over the top of each apple, then wrap the foil securely around the apples to enclose them.
4. Bake for about 35 minutes, or until cooked. Serve with yoghurt or cream.

bread and butter pudding

SERVES 4

butter, for greasing

6 slices bread

750 ml (26 fl oz/3 cups) milk

1/4 teaspoon lemon zest

110 g (3 3/4 oz/1/2 cup) sugar

4 eggs

125 g (4 1/2 oz/2/3 cup) dried mixed fruits (sultanas/golden raisins, raisins, chopped dried apricots, currants, mixed peel/mixed candied citrus peel)

1. Preheat the oven to 180°C (350°F/Gas 4). Grease a large ovenproof dish or four small dishes. Butter the bread and cut off the crusts.
2. Heat the milk in a saucepan and add the lemon zest. Bring to the boil, then cover and remove from the heat, leaving the milk to infuse for 10 minutes. Beat the sugar and eggs together, then strain the milk over the eggs and mix well.
3. Scatter half the dried fruit over the bottom of the dish and arrange half the bread, buttered sides down, on top. Pour in half the custard, then repeat with the remaining fruit, bread and custard.
4. Put the ovenproof dish or dishes in a large roasting tin. Pour water into the tin to come halfway up the side of the dish (this is called a bain-marie). Bake for 35 minutes.

fruit jelly

MAKES 6

1 tablespoon gelatine powder

375 ml (13 fl oz/1½ cups) unsweetened fruit juice

200 g (7 oz/¾ cup) puréed fresh or drained, tinned fruit in natural juice

1. Sprinkle the gelatine over 125 ml (4 fl oz/½ cup) of cool water in a small saucepan. Heat through, then add the fruit juice and heat again.
2. Pour into a mixing bowl and leave until it begins to thicken. Stir in the puréed fruit until well combined.
3. Transfer to six small dishes or glasses and refrigerate until set.

choc-honeycomb mousse

SERVES 4

150 ml (5½ fl oz) cream

300 g (10½ oz) good-quality dark or milk chocolate, chopped

3 eggs, separated

2 chocolate-coated honeycomb bars, crumbled

1 Pour the cream into a heavy-based saucepan over medium heat. Remove from the heat just before the cream begins to boil.

2 Add the chopped chocolate, stirring until the chocolate has melted and the mixture is well combined. Pour into a large mixing bowl and set aside to cool for a few minutes.

3 Using electric beaters, beat the egg yolks into the chocolate mixture and continue beating for 1–2 minutes, or until the mixture has thickened.

4 Put the egg whites into a clean bowl and whisk until stiff peaks form. Gently fold into the chocolate mixture with a large flat metal spoon. Spoon into four 125 ml (4 fl oz/½ cup) ramekins and refrigerate overnight to set. Serve with the honeycomb bars on top.

lemon cheesecakes

MAKES 12

250 g (9 oz) honey snap or granita biscuits

1½ teaspoons mixed (pumpkin pie) spice

125 g (4½ oz) unsalted butter, melted

filling

375 g (13 oz) cream cheese

1 tablespoon grated lemon zest

2 teaspoons vanilla extract

400 g (14 oz) tinned sweetened condensed milk

4 tablespoons lemon juice

1. Grease 12 standard muffin holes with melted butter or oil. Line each hole with two strips of baking paper.
2. Put the biscuits in a food processor and process until finely crushed. Add the spice and melted butter and process to combine.
3. Press half the crumb mixture into the bases of the muffin holes. Press the remainder around the sides of the holes. Use a flat-bottomed glass to press the crumbs firmly into place. Put in the fridge.
4. To make the filling, beat the cream cheese with electric beaters until smooth and creamy. Add the lemon zest and vanilla extract. Mix well. Gradually beat in the condensed milk and lemon juice. Beat for 5 minutes, or until the mixture is smooth.
5. Pour the filling into the crumb cases and smooth the tops. Refrigerate the cheesecakes overnight. Lift out of the muffin holes, using the baking paper handles.

jam pudding

SERVES 6

160 g (5 3/4 oz/1/2 cup) strawberry jam

60 g (2 1/4 oz) unsalted butter

115 g (4 oz/1/2 cup) caster (superfine) sugar

1 egg

225 g (8 oz/1 3/4 cups) plain (all-purpose) flour

1 teaspoon baking powder

125 ml (4 fl oz/1/2 cup) milk

1 Grease six individual pudding bowls or a 1 litre (35 fl oz/4 cup) pudding bowl with butter. Spread the jam in the base.

2 Beat the butter, sugar and egg until smooth and creamy. Sift in the flour and baking powder. Add the milk and mix well. Spread the batter carefully on top of the jam in the pudding bowls.

3 Make a foil lid for each bowl. Press around the edges to seal tight. Make string handles for the bowls.

4 Put the pudding bowls into a large pan. Pour enough hot water into the pan to come a third of the way up the bowls. Put the lid on the pan and place over low heat. Simmer for 1 hour. Keep refilling with water.

5 Run a knife around the edge of each pudding. Tip onto a serving plate. Serve.

lemon delicious

SERVES 4

60 g (2¼ oz) unsalted butter
170 g (6 oz/¾ cup) caster (superfine) sugar
3 eggs, separated
1 teaspoon grated lemon zest
40 g (1½ oz/⅓ cup) self-raising flour
185 ml (6 fl oz/¾ cup) milk
3 tablespoons lemon juice

1. Preheat the oven to 180°C (350°F/Gas 4). Lightly grease a 1 litre (35 fl oz/4 cup) ovenproof dish or four individual dishes with a little melted butter.
2. Beat the butter, sugar, egg yolks and lemon zest in a large bowl until the mixture is light and creamy. Fold in the flour, milk and lemon juice.
3. Beat the egg whites in a bowl until soft peaks form. Fold into the butter and sugar mixture, then pour into the dish. Bake for 30–40 minutes, or until golden.

tangy lime delicious

SERVES 4

30 g (1 oz) butter
250 g (9 oz/1 cup) sugar
1 tablespoon grated lime zest
2 eggs, separated
40 g (1½ oz/⅓ cup) self-raising flour
150 ml (5 fl oz) skim milk
125 ml (4 fl oz/½ cup) lime juice

1. Preheat the oven to 180°C (350°F/Gas 4). Lightly grease a 1 litre (35 fl oz/4 cup) ovenproof dish or four individual dishes with a little melted butter.
2. Beat the butter, sugar and lime zest in a bowl until the mixture is light and creamy. Gradually add the egg yolks, beating well between each addition.
3. Fold in the flour, milk and lime juice. Beat the egg whites in a bowl until soft peaks form. Fold into the butter and sugar mixture, then pour into the dish. Bake for 30–40 minutes, or until golden.

pancakes

MAKES ABOUT 12

125 g (4½ oz/1 cup) plain (all-purpose) flour
sprinkle of salt
1 egg
310 ml (10¾ fl oz/1¼ cups) milk
lemon juice and sugar, to sprinkle
cream or ice cream, to serve

1. Sift the flour and salt into a mixing bowl and make a well in the centre.
2. Add the egg and milk. Whisk until smooth. Set aside for 1 hour.
3. Gently heat a lightly greased 20 cm (8 inch) frying pan. Pour about 3 tablespoons of batter into the pan. Tilt the pan to spread the batter evenly.
4. Lift the edges with a knife. When golden, flip the pancake over and cook the other side.
5. Sprinkle lemon juice and sugar over the pancake. Roll up and serve hot with whipped cream or ice cream, if desired.

sticky date pudding

SERVES 6

45 g (1½ oz/½ cup) desiccated coconut

115 g (4 oz/½ cup) soft brown sugar

90 g (3¼ oz/¾ cup) self-raising flour

30 g (1 oz/¼ cup) plain (all-purpose) flour

½ teaspoon bicarbonate of soda (baking soda)

100 g (3½ oz) unsalted butter

90 g (3 oz/¼ cup) golden syrup or honey

185 g (6½ oz/1 cup) chopped dates

3 tablespoons orange juice

2 eggs, lightly beaten

sauce

80 g (2¾ oz) unsalted butter

55 g (2 oz/¼ cup) soft brown sugar

250 ml (9 fl oz/1 cup) cream

2 tablespoons golden syrup or honey

1. Preheat the oven to 180°C (350°F/Gas 4). Brush six small pudding bowls with melted butter or oil.
2. Combine 2 tablespoons each of the coconut and brown sugar and sprinkle into the bowls.
3. Sift the flours and soda into a mixing bowl. Add the remaining coconut and make a well in the centre.
4. Combine the remaining sugar, butter, golden syrup, dates and orange juice in a saucepan. Stir over medium heat until the butter melts.
5. Using a metal spoon, fold the date mixture into the dry ingredients. Add the eggs and stir until smooth.
6. Pour the mixture into the bowls and bake for 35 minutes. Leave the puddings in the bowls for 5 minutes before turning out.
7. To make the sauce, combine all the ingredients in a saucepan. Stir over low heat until the sugar and butter have dissolved. Stir for a further 2 minutes, then serve over the hot pudding.

upside-down banana cake

SERVES 6

125 g (4½ oz) unsalted butter

185 g (6½ oz/¾ cup) caster (superfine) sugar

1 egg

250 g (9 oz/2 cups) plain (all-purpose) flour

2 teaspoons baking powder

185 ml (6 fl oz/¾ cup) milk

1 large banana, mashed

75 g (2½ oz) unsalted butter, melted

95 g (3¼ oz/½ cup) soft brown sugar

260 g (9¼ oz/1 cup) tinned crushed pineapple, drained

cream, to serve

1. Preheat the oven to 180°C (350°F/Gas 4). Grease six small spring-form cake tins or a 20 cm (8 inch) spring-form cake tin.
2. Beat the butter, sugar and egg until smooth. Sift in the flour and baking powder. Mix well, then add the milk and mashed banana.
3. Spread the melted butter in the base of each tin, then sprinkle evenly with the brown sugar.
4. Spread the crushed pineapple over the sugar. Pour the batter evenly over the top. Bake for 40–45 minutes.
5. Tip out onto a plate. Serve warm with cream.

caramel sauce

SERVES 6–8

100 g (3½ oz) unsalted butter

185 g (6½ oz/1 cup) soft brown sugar

125 ml (4 fl oz/½ cup) cream

1 Combine all the ingredients in a small saucepan. Stir over medium heat until the mixture is smooth. Bring to the boil, reduce the heat slightly and simmer for 2 minutes.

strawberry sauce

SERVES 8

250 g (9 oz) strawberries

2 tablespoons caster (superfine) sugar

1 tablespoon orange or lemon juice

1 Put the strawberries, sugar and juice into a blender and blend until the mixture is smooth. Chill in the refrigerator.

hot choc sauce

SERVES 6–8

250 g (9 oz) dark chocolate

170 ml (5½ fl oz/⅔ cup) cream

2 tablespoons golden syrup or honey

40 g (1½ oz) unsalted butter

1 Chop the chocolate roughly. Place the chocolate, cream, syrup and butter in a saucepan. Stir over low heat until the chocolate has melted and the mixture is smooth. Serve immediately.

banana split

SERVES 4

4 large ripe bananas, halved lengthways

8 small scoops vanilla ice cream

sauce of your choice

mixed lollies, to decorate

12 small white or pink marshmallows

40 g (1½ oz/¼ cup) crushed nuts

1 Arrange the two halves of each banana in a long, shallow serving dish and top with two scoops of ice cream.

2 Pour over the sauce of your choice. Decorate with the lollies, marshmallows and crushed nuts and serve immediately.

biscuits, cakes and fetes

chocolate brownies

MAKES ABOUT 30

40 g (1½ oz/⅓ cup) plain (all-purpose) flour

60 g (2¼ oz/½ cup) dark cocoa powder

440 g (15½ oz/2 cups) sugar

125 g (4½ oz/1 cup) chopped pecans or pistachios

250 g (9 oz) dark chocolate, chopped

250 g (9 oz) unsalted butter, melted

2 teaspoons vanilla extract

4 eggs, lightly beaten

1. Preheat the oven to 180°C (350°F/Gas 4). Grease and line a 20 x 30 cm (8 x 12 inch) rectangular cake tin. Sift the flour and cocoa into a large bowl, add the sugar and nuts and mix well. Stir in the chocolate and make a well in the centre.
2. Add the butter, vanilla and eggs. Stir until combined.
3. Pour the mixture into the tin and smooth the surface. Bake for 45 minutes. Cool in the tin before cutting into squares.

chocolate chip cookies

MAKES ABOUT 22

185 g (6½ oz/1½ cups) plain (all-purpose) flour

125 g (4½ oz/1 cup) unsweetened cocoa powder

280 g (10 oz/1½ cups) soft brown sugar

180 g (6½ oz) unsalted butter

150 g (5½ oz) dark chocolate, chopped

3 eggs, lightly beaten

170 g (6 oz/1 cup) dark choc chips

50 g (1¾ oz/⅓ cup) white choc chips

150 g (5½ oz) nuts of your choice, chopped (such as macadamias, pecans, almonds, brazils, walnuts or pistachios)

1 Preheat the oven to 180°C (350°F/Gas 4). Line two baking trays with baking paper.

2 Sift the flour and cocoa into a bowl and stir in the sugar. Make a well in the centre.

3 Heat the butter and chocolate in a saucepan over low heat. Stir until the mixture is smooth.

4 Stir the butter mixture and eggs into the dry ingredients. Mix until well combined. Stir in the dark and white choc chips and the nuts.

5 Drop heaped tablespoons of the mixture onto the trays. Flatten each one slightly with your fingertips.

6 Bake for 15 minutes. Leave on the trays for at least 5 minutes before transferring to a wire rack to cool.

gingerbread people

MAKES ABOUT 16

125 g (4½ oz) unsalted butter

95 g (3¼ oz/½ cup) soft brown sugar

115 g (4 oz/⅓ cup) golden syrup or honey

1 egg

250 g (9 oz/2 cups) plain (all-purpose) flour

40 g (1½ oz/⅓ cup) self-raising flour

1 tablespoon ground ginger

1 teaspoon bicarbonate of soda (baking soda)

icing

1 egg white

½ teaspoon lemon juice

125 g (4½ oz/1 cup) icing (confectioners') sugar

assorted food colourings

1 Line two baking trays with baking paper. Beat the butter, sugar and syrup in a bowl until light and creamy. Add the egg and beat well. Sift in the flours, ginger and soda. Use a knife to mix until combined.

2 Gather the dough into two balls. Knead on a floured surface until smooth. Roll out the dough between two sheets of baking paper to a 5 mm (¼ inch) thickness. Refrigerate for 30 minutes. Preheat the oven to 180°C (350°F/Gas 4).

3 Cut the dough into people, using cutters. Press any remaining dough together. Re-roll and cut out into shapes. Bake for 10 minutes, or until browned. Once cool, decorate with the icing.

4 To make the icing, beat the egg white in a bowl with electric beaters until soft peaks form. Add the lemon juice and icing sugar and beat until thick and creamy.

5 Divide the icing into bowls and tint with the food colourings. Spoon into paper icing bags and use to decorate the biscuits.

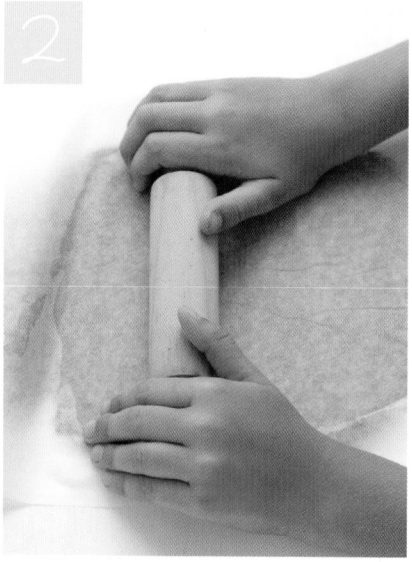

anzac biscuits

MAKES ABOUT 25

200 g (7 oz/2 cups) rolled (porridge) oats

125 g (4½ oz/1 cup) plain (all-purpose) flour

180 g (6½ oz/2 cups) desiccated coconut

350 g (12 oz/1½ cups) caster (superfine) sugar

250 g (9 oz) unsalted butter

4 tablespoons golden syrup or honey

1 teaspoon bicarbonate of soda (baking soda)

1. Preheat the oven to 160°C (315°F/Gas 2–3). Lightly grease two baking trays. Put the oats, flour, coconut and sugar in a large mixing bowl.
2. Melt the butter and golden syrup in a saucepan, stirring. Take off the heat.
3. Mix the baking soda and 2 tablespoons of boiling water in a cup. Add to the melted butter in the saucepan. Add to the bowl and mix well to combine.
4. Roll tablespoons of the mixture into balls. Put on trays spacing them 5 cm (2 inches) apart. Press lightly with a fork. Bake for 20 minutes, one tray at a time, until golden and crisp.

melting moments

MAKES ABOUT 45

40 g (1½ oz/⅓ cup) cornflour (cornstarch)

125 g (4½ oz/1 cup) plain (all-purpose) flour

180 g (6½ oz) unsalted butter

40 g (1½ oz/⅓ cup) icing (confectioners') sugar

1 teaspoon vanilla extract

100 g (3½ oz) glacé cherries, halved

1. Preheat the oven to 180°C (350°F/Gas 4). Line two baking trays with baking paper.
2. Sift the cornflour and plain flour into a bowl.
3. Put the butter, sugar and vanilla into a mixing bowl and beat with electric beaters until light and creamy.
4. Using a flat-bladed knife, stir the sifted flours into the butter mixture until just combined and the mixture is smooth.
5. Spoon teaspoons of the mixture onto the trays, leaving room for spreading.
6. Top each biscuit with half a cherry and bake for 15 minutes, or until lightly golden and crisp.
7. Transfer the biscuits to a wire rack to cool.

muesli slice

MAKES 18 SLICES

250 g (9 oz) unsalted butter
230 g (8 oz/1 cup) caster (superfine) sugar
2 tablespoons honey
250 g (9 oz/2 1/2 cups) rolled (porridge) oats
65 g (2 1/4 oz/3/4 cup) desiccated coconut
30 g (1 oz/1 cup) cornflakes, lightly crushed
45 g (1 1/2 oz/1/2 cup) flaked almonds
1 teaspoon mixed (pumpkin pie) spice
90 g (3 1/4 oz/1/2 cup) finely chopped dried apricots
125 g (4 1/2 oz/1 cup) plain (all-purpose) flour
180 g (6 1/2 oz/1 cup) dried mixed fruit

1. Preheat the oven to 160°C (315°F/Gas 2–3). Brush a shallow 23 cm (9 inch) square cake tin with melted butter or oil. Line with baking paper.
2. Put the butter, sugar and honey in a small saucepan and stir over low heat until the butter has melted and the sugar has dissolved.
3. Put the oats, coconut, cornflakes, almonds, spice, apricots, flour and mixed fruit into a large mixing bowl and mix until well combined. Make a well in the centre.
4. Add the butter and sugar mixture and mix until well combined. Put into the tin.
5. Bake for 30–45 minutes, or until golden. Using a sharp knife, cut lines in the slice to divide it up into 18 pieces but do not cut right through to the base. Leave in the tin for 15 minutes before turning it out onto a board to cool. Cut into bars when cold.

caramel slice

MAKES 18–20 SLICES

60 g (2¼ oz/½ cup) plain (all-purpose) flour

60 g (2¼ oz/½ cup) self-raising flour

90 g (3¼ oz/1 cup) desiccated coconut

100 g (3½ oz) unsalted butter

115 g (4 oz/½ cup) soft brown sugar

filling

30 g (1 oz) unsalted butter

2 tablespoons golden syrup or honey

400 g (14 oz) sweetened condensed milk

topping

150 g (5½ oz) dark chocolate, roughly chopped

40 g (1½ oz) unsalted butter

1 Preheat the oven to 180°C (350°F/Gas 4). Line a shallow 28 x 18 cm (11¼ x 7 inch) baking tin. Sift the flours together into a bowl. Stir in the coconut and make a well in the centre.

2 Combine the butter and sugar in a saucepan and stir over low heat until the butter has melted. Pour into the dry ingredients and stir well to combine.

3 Press the mixture evenly into the tin with the back of a spoon. Bake for 10 minutes, then leave to cool.

4 To make the filling, combine the butter, syrup and condensed milk in a saucepan. Stir over low heat until smooth. Continue stirring for 10 minutes. Pour over the pastry base and bake for 20 minutes.

5 To make the topping, place the chocolate and butter in a heatproof bowl over a saucepan of barely simmering water. Stir until smooth.

6 Spread over the caramel and leave to set. Lift the slice from the tin and cut into bars or squares to serve.

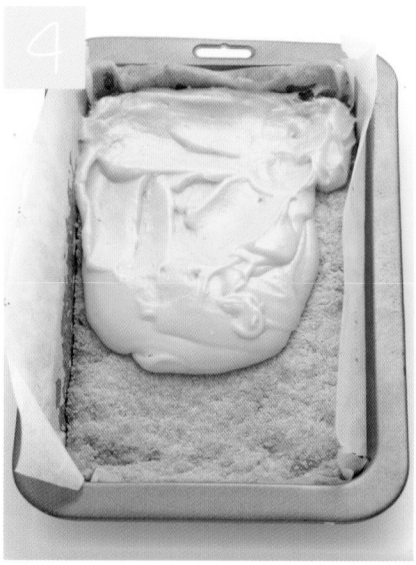

jam drops

MAKES ABOUT 32

80 g (2 3/4 oz) unsalted butter
80 g (2 3/4 oz/1/3 cup) caster (superfine) sugar
2 tablespoons milk
1/2 teaspoon vanilla extract
125 g (4 1/2 oz/1 cup) self-raising flour
40 g (1 1/2 oz/1/3 cup) custard powder
2 tablespoons strawberry jam

1. Preheat the oven to 180°C (350°F/Gas 4). Line two baking trays with baking paper.
2. Using electric beaters, beat the butter and sugar in a small bowl until the mixture is light and creamy. Add the milk and vanilla and beat until combined.
3. Sift the flour and custard powder into the butter mixture and mix to form a soft dough.
4. Roll 2 teaspoons of the mixture at a time into balls and place on the baking trays.
5. Press a hollow in each ball with your thumb or the end of a wooden spoon and fill each hole with 1/4 teaspoon of jam.
6. Bake the biscuits for 15 minutes, then transfer to a wire rack to cool.

rocky road

MAKES ABOUT 36 PIECES

25 g (1 oz/1/4 cup) desiccated coconut
100 g (3 1/2 oz) white marshmallows
100 g (3 1/2 oz) pink marshmallows
70 g (2 1/2 oz/1/2 cup) unsalted mixed nuts
60 g (2 1/4 oz/1/4 cup) glacé cherries, halved
375 g (13 oz) dark chocolate melts (buttons)

1. Line a shallow 28 x 18 cm (11 1/4 x 7 inch) cake tin with foil. Sprinkle half the coconut over the base of the tin.
2. Cut the marshmallows in half and arrange in the tin, alternating colours and leaving a little space between the pieces. Sprinkle the remaining coconut, nuts and cherries in the spaces between the marshmallows and around the edge of the tin.
3. Place the chocolate in a heatproof bowl. Put the bowl over a saucepan of simmering water and stir until the chocolate has melted. Cool slightly. Pour over the marshmallow mixture.
4. Tap the tin gently on the bench to settle the chocolate. Leave to set. When firm, cut into pieces with a sharp knife.

coconut ice

MAKES 30 PIECES

310 g (11 oz/2½ cups) icing (confectioners') sugar

¼ teaspoon cream of tartar

1 egg white, lightly beaten

3 tablespoons condensed milk

155 g (5½ oz/1¾ cups) desiccated coconut

pink food colouring

1. Brush a bar tin with melted butter or oil. Line with baking paper and grease the paper. Sift the icing sugar and cream of tartar into a bowl. Make a well in the centre.
2. Add the combined egg white and condensed milk. Stir in the coconut. Mix until well combined. Divide the mixture between two bowls. Tint the contents of one bowl with pink colouring. Knead the colour through evenly.
3. Press the pink mixture into the base of the tin. Cover with the white mixture and press down gently. Refrigerate for 1 hour, or until set.
4. When firm, remove from the tin and cut into squares.

chocolate cake

SERVES 8–10

125 g (4½ oz) unsalted butter

170 g (6 oz/¾ cup) caster (superfine) sugar

3 eggs

1 tablespoon golden syrup or honey

1 teaspoon vanilla extract

185 g (6½ oz/1½ cups) plain (all-purpose) flour

½ teaspoon baking powder

¼ tablespoon bicarbonate of soda (baking soda)

3 tablespoons unsweetened cocoa powder

125 ml (4 fl oz/½ cup) milk

icing

125 g (4½ oz/1 cup) icing (confectioners') sugar

1½ tablespoons unsweetened cocoa powder

20 g (¾ oz) unsalted butter, softened

1. Preheat the oven to 180°C (350°F/Gas 4). Grease a 20 cm (8 inch) spring-form cake tin. Line with baking paper. Beat the butter, sugar and eggs until smooth and creamy.
2. Stir in the golden syrup and vanilla. Sift in the flour, baking powder, bicarbonate of soda and cocoa. Mix in the milk.
3. Spread evenly in the tin. Bake for 45–55 minutes.
4. Leave to stand for 10 minutes, then take out of the tin. Cool completely.
5. To make the icing, mix the icing sugar, cocoa and butter with a litle hot water. When smooth, spread over the cake.

scones

MAKES 12

250 g (9 oz/2 cups) self-raising flour

pinch of salt

30 g (1 oz) unsalted butter

185 ml (6 fl oz/3/4 cup) milk or buttermilk

extra milk, for glazing

butter or jam and whipped cream, to serve

1 Preheat the oven to 210°C (415°F/Gas 6–7). Brush a baking tray with melted butter or oil.

2 Sift the flour and salt into a large bowl. Add the butter and rub it in lightly using your fingertips until it looks like fine breadcrumbs.

3 Make a well in the centre. Add almost all the milk and mix with a flat-bladed knife to a soft dough, adding more milk if necessary.

4 Turn the dough out onto a lightly floured surface and knead briefly until smooth. Roll out the dough to 1–2 cm (1/2–3/4 inches) thick. Cut into 12 rounds with a 5 cm (2 inch) cutter.

5 Place the rounds close together on the tray. Brush the tops with a little extra milk. Bake for 10–15 minutes, or until golden brown. Serve with butter, or jam and whipped cream.

meringues

MAKES 35

3 egg whites

115 g (4 oz/1/2 cup) caster (superfine) sugar

40 g (1 1/2 oz/1/3 cup) icing (confectioners') sugar

1/2 tablespoon cream of tartar

1. Preheat the oven to 150°C (300°F/Gas 2). Line a baking tray with baking paper.
2. Beat the egg whites until stiff. Gradually blend in the caster sugar until thick and glossy.
3. Fold in the icing sugar and cream of tartar. Spoon or pipe small mounds onto the tray.
4. Reduce the oven to 100°C (200°F/Gas 1/2). Bake for 45–55 minutes, or until dry.

carrot cake with ricotta topping

SERVES 12–14

310 g (11 oz/2½ cups) self-raising flour

1 teaspoon bicarbonate of soda (baking soda)

2 teaspoons ground cinnamon

1 teaspoon mixed (pumpkin pie) spice

90 g (3¼ oz/½ cup) soft brown sugar

60 g (2¼ oz/½ cup) sultanas (golden raisins)

2 eggs, lightly beaten

2 tablespoons canola oil

4 tablespoons milk

140 g (5 oz/½ cup) apple purée

300 g (10½ oz) carrots, coarsely grated

ricotta topping

125 g (4½ oz/½ cup) ricotta cheese

30 g (1 oz/¼ cup) icing (confectioners') sugar

1 teaspoon grated lime zest

1 Preheat the oven to 180°C (350°F/Gas 4). Lightly grease a 10 x 18 cm (4 x 7 inch) loaf (bar) tin and line the base with baking paper. Sift the flour, bicarbonate soda and spices into a large bowl. Stir in the brown sugar and sultanas.

2 Combine the eggs, oil, milk and apple purée. Stir the egg mixture into the flour mixture.

3 Add the carrot and mix well to combine. Spread into the tin and bake for 1 hour 15 minutes, or until the cake comes away slightly from the sides. Leave for 5 minutes, then turn out onto a wire rack.

4 To make the topping, beat the ricotta, icing sugar and lime zest together until smooth. Spread over the cooled cake.

cupcakes

MAKES ABOUT 18

250 g (9 oz/2 cups) self-raising flour

165 g (5¾ oz/¾ cup) sugar

125 g (4½ oz) unsalted butter, softened

3 eggs

3 tablespoons milk

½ teaspoon vanilla extract

icing

90 g (3¼ oz/¾ cup) icing (confectioners') sugar

1 teaspoon unsweetened cocoa powder

20 g (¾ oz) unsalted butter, softened

chocolate melts (buttons), to decorate

1. Preheat the oven to 180°C (350°F/Gas 4). Put 18 paper patty cases in standard muffin holes.
2. Sift the flour and sugar into a mixing bowl. Add the butter, eggs, milk and vanilla and beat until smooth. Fill the patty cases three-quarters full with the mixture.
3. Bake for 15 minutes, or until the cupcakes are golden. Cool on a wire rack.
4. To make the icing, mix the icing sugar, cocoa and butter with a little hot water until smooth. Spread over the cakes. Top each cake with a chocolate melt.

lemon butterfly cakes

MAKES 18

250 g (9 oz/2 cups) self-raising flour
165 g (5¾ oz/¾ cup) sugar
125 g (4½ oz) unsalted butter, softened
3 eggs
3 tablespoons milk
½ teaspoon vanilla extract
2 teaspoons grated lemon zest
170 g (6 oz/⅔ cup) lemon butter curd
125 ml (4 fl oz/½ cup) cream
18 silver balls

1. Preheat the oven to 180°C (350°F/Gas 4). Put 18 paper patty cases in standard muffin holes.
2. Sift the flour and sugar into a bowl. Add the butter, eggs, milk and vanilla and beat until smooth. Mix in the zest. Fill the patty cases three-quarters full with the mixture. Bake for 15 minutes, or until golden.
3. Cut a circle from the top of each cake. Cut the circles in half. Put ½ teaspoon of lemon butter into each cake.
4. Beat the cream until firm peaks form. Put 1 tablespoon of cream onto each cake. Press the half-circles on top to form 'wings'. Decorate with silver balls.

apple and orange mini cakes

MAKES 24

90 g (3¼ oz) unsalted butter

125 g (4½ oz/⅔ cup) soft brown sugar

1 tablespoon honey

1 egg

270 g (9½ oz/1 cup) apple purée

125 g (4½ oz/1 cup) wholemeal (whole-wheat) self-raising flour

60 g (2¼ oz/½ cup) self-raising flour

1 teaspoon ground cinnamon

pinch of powdered cloves

orange glaze icing

125 g (4½ oz/1 cup) icing (confectioners') sugar

10 g (¼ oz) unsalted butter

1 teaspoon grated orange zest

2 tablespoons orange juice

1 Preheat the oven to 180°C (350°F/Gas 4). Grease 24 mini muffin holes. Beat the butter, sugar and honey together until light and creamy, then add the egg and apple purée and beat until well combined.

2 Sift in the flours and spices and mix well. Spoon the mixture into the muffin holes and bake for 20 minutes. Allow to cool.

3 To make the icing, mix the icing sugar, butter, orange zest and orange juice in a heatproof bowl. Place over a saucepan of simmering water and stir until smooth. Allow to cool slightly, then ice the cakes.

let's party

zebra sandwiches

MAKES 6

8 slices white bread

20 g (3/4 oz) butter

2 tablespoons Vegemite, Marmite or
4 tablespoons hazelnut spread

1. Spread three slices of bread with butter and Vegemite, Marmite or hazelnut spread. Stack the slices, spread side up. Top with the unbuttered slice. Press down gently. Do the same with the other four slices of bread.
2. Remove the crusts with a sharp knife and cut each stack into three fingers.

banana and date fingers

MAKES 18

20 g (3/4 oz) butter

12 slices white bread

3 bananas, mashed

6 fresh dates, chopped

1. Butter the bread and spread six slices with mashed banana and top with dates. Top with the remaining six slices of bread to make sandwiches.
2. Remove the crusts with a sharp knife and cut each sandwich into three fingers.

mini burgers

MAKES 10 SMALL OR 20 MINI

500 g (1 lb 2 oz) minced (ground) beef

1 small onion, finely chopped

1 tablespoon finely chopped flat-leaf (Italian) parsley

1 egg, lightly beaten

1 tablespoon tomato sauce (ketchup)

2 tablespoons oil

1/2 lettuce, finely shredded

2 small tomatoes, thinly sliced

10 small bread rolls or 20 mini dinner rolls, cut in half

80 g (2 3/4 oz) cheddar cheese, thinly sliced

5 tinned pineapple rings, drained and quartered

tomato sauce (ketchup) or barbecue sauce, to serve

1. Combine the beef, onion, parsley, beaten egg and tomato sauce in a large bowl. Using your hands, mix until well combined.
2. Divide the mixture into 10 portions or 20 smaller portions. Shape into round patties.
3. Heat the oil in a large, heavy-based frying pan over medium heat. Cook the patties for 5 minutes on each side, or until they are well browned and cooked through. Remove and drain on paper towels.
4. To assemble the burgers, put lettuce and tomato on the base of each roll. Top with a meat patty, cheese slice and pineapple piece. Add the sauce and cover with the top of the roll. Serve immediately.

baked potato wedges

SERVES 4

1.3 kg (3 lb) orange sweet potato

2 tablespoons olive oil

1. Preheat the oven to 200°C (400°F/Gas 6). Peel and slice the orange sweet potato into wedges.
2. Put the wedges in a large roasting tin and toss with the olive oil. Bake for about 30 minutes, or until browned and crisp. Serve warm.

baked chicken nuggets

SERVES 4

40 g (1½ oz/1⅓ cups) cornflakes

400 g (14 oz) boneless, skinless chicken breasts

plain (all-purpose) flour, for dusting

1 egg white, lightly beaten

1. Preheat the oven to 200°C (400°F/Gas 6). Put the cornflakes in a food processor and process to fine crumbs.
2. Cut the chicken breasts into bite-sized pieces. Toss in seasoned flour, then in the egg white. Roll each piece in the cornflake crumbs until well coated.
3. Lightly grease a baking tray with oil and place the nuggets on it. Bake for 10 minutes, or until golden and cooked through.

frankfurt bonbons

MAKES 12

12 small good-quality cocktail frankfurts
3 sheets frozen puff pastry, thawed
1 egg, lightly beaten
cotton or jute string

1. Preheat the oven to 180°C (350°F/Gas 4). Line two baking trays with baking paper.
2. Prick the frankfurts with a fork. Cut each pastry sheet into four squares. Brush each square with beaten egg.
3. Place a frankfurt on each pastry square and roll it up. Gently press the edges together.
4. Carefully pinch in the ends of the pastry. Tie the ends loosely with pieces of string.
5. Place the pastries on the trays. Brush lightly with the beaten egg. Bake for 15 minutes, or until golden. Remind your party guests not to eat the string!

animal crisps

MAKES 20

1 sheet frozen puff pastry, thawed

1 egg, lightly beaten

30 g (1 oz/1/4 cup) grated cheddar cheese

1. Preheat the oven to 180°C (350°F/Gas 4). Line a baking tray with baking paper.
2. Cut animal shapes out of the pastry using assorted biscuit (cookie) cutters. Place on the tray.
3. Brush with the egg. Sprinkle the shapes with cheese. Bake for 10–15 minutes, or until golden and crisp.

caramel popcorn balls

MAKES 50

2 tablespoons oil

1/2 cup popping corn

170 g (6 oz/3/4 cup) caster (superfine) sugar

80 g (2 3/4 oz) unsalted butter

2 tablespoons honey

2 tablespoons cream

1. Heat the oil in a large saucepan over medium heat. Add the corn and cover with a lid. Cook for 5 minutes, or until the popping stops, shaking the pan occasionally. Tip the popcorn into a big bowl.
2. Put the sugar, butter, honey and cream in a small saucepan. Stir over medium heat, without boiling, until the sugar has completely dissolved. Bring to the boil and boil, without stirring, for 5 minutes.
3. Pour the caramel over the popcorn and mix together. Leave to cool a little, then rub some oil over your hands and mould the popcorn into small balls. Put on a wire rack to set.

baby choc éclairs

MAKES ABOUT 24

75 g (2½ oz) unsalted butter
125 g (4½ oz/1 cup) plain (all-purpose) flour
4 eggs
125 g (4½ oz) dark chocolate, melted
whipped cream, to serve

1. Preheat the oven to 200°C (400°F/Gas 6). Line a baking tray with baking paper. Put the butter in a saucepan and add 250 ml (9 fl oz/1 cup) of water. Bring to the boil. Sift in all the flour. Cook, stirring, until the mixture forms a ball. Leave to cool for 5 minutes.
2. Add the eggs, one at a time, beating well until thick and glossy. Spoon into a piping bag and pipe short lengths onto the baking tray. Sprinkle with a little water.
3. Bake for 10–15 minutes. Reduce the oven to 180°C (350°F/Gas 4) and bake for a further 10–15 minutes, or until golden and firm.
4. Pierce the side of each éclair with a skewer to allow steam to escape. Turn off the oven and return the eclairs to the oven for about 5 minutes to dry out. Cool on a wire rack.
5. Split the éclairs in half lengthways and remove any uncooked pastry. Spread the tops with chocolate, leave to set, fill with cream and replace the tops.

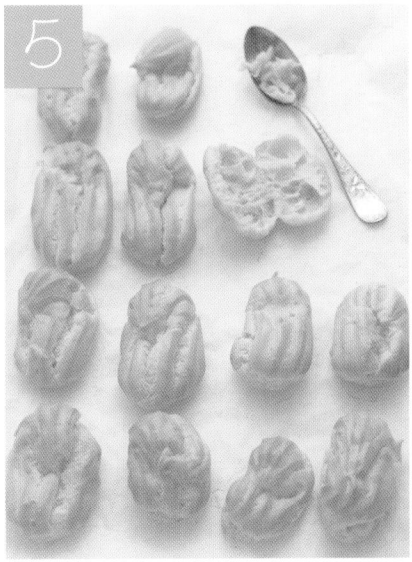

pecan tarts

MAKES 8

8 frozen shortcrust pastry cases

30 g (1 oz/1/4 cup) self-raising flour

1/2 teaspoon mixed (pumpkin pie) spice

85 g (3 oz/2/3 cup) chopped pecan nuts

1 egg, lightly beaten

1 tablespoon milk

2 tablespoons golden syrup or honey

1/2 teaspoon vanilla extract

1. Preheat the oven to 190°C (375°F/ Gas 5). Arrange the pastry cases on a baking tray.
2. Sift the flour and spice into a bowl. Stir in the nuts. Make a well in the centre.
3. Add the egg, milk, golden syrup and vanilla. Beat with a fork until almost smooth.
4. Spoon the filling evenly into the pastry cases. Bake on the top shelf of the oven for 15 minutes. Allow to cool on a wire rack.

beach baby jellies

MAKES 12

2 x 85 g (3 oz) packets green jelly crystals
2 tablespoons fine biscuit (cookie) crumbs
12 jelly babies
12 lifesavers sweets
12 paper parasols

1. Combine the jelly crystals and 500 ml (17 fl oz/ 2 cups) of boiling water in a bowl. Stir until all the crystals have dissolved. Set aside until cool. Pour the jelly into small moulds to three-quarters full. Refrigerate overnight.
2. Sprinkle the biscuit crumbs over half of each jelly. Lay a jelly baby on the crumbs. Place a lifesaver on the crumbs and put a paper parasol through the centre.

bleeding fingers

MAKES 20

2 egg whites

110 g (3 3/4 oz/1/2 cup) sugar

90 g (3 1/4 oz/1 cup) desiccated coconut

160 g (5 3/4 oz/1/2 cup) raspberry or strawberry jam

10 coloured jellybeans

1. Preheat the oven to 150°C (300°F/Gas 2). Line a baking tray with baking paper.
2. Beat the egg whites until stiff peaks form. Beat in the sugar, 1 tablespoon at a time, and continue beating until the mixture becomes thick and glossy. Fold through the coconut.
3. Fill a piping bag fitted with a plain 2 cm (3/4 inch) nozzle with the meringue mixture. Pipe 20 x 8 cm (3 1/4 inch) lengths onto the tray.
4. Bake for 5 minutes. Reduce the heat to 120°C (235°F/Gas 1/2) and bake for a further 45–50 minutes, or until the meringues are light and crisp. Turn off the oven and leave the meringues to cool.
5. Heat the jam in a saucepan over low heat until thin and runny. Pour into a bowl. Cut one end from each jellybean and discard the end. Cut the remaining jellybeans in half lengthways. Press the jellybean on the end of each meringue. Drizzle with warm jam to resemble the blood.

blood baths

MAKES 12

300 g (10 1/2 oz) frozen raspberries

3 sheets frozen puff pastry, thawed

30 g (1 oz/1/4 cup) icing (confectioners') sugar, sifted

1. Place the raspberries in a bowl. Allow to stand for 10–15 minutes, or until thawed slightly. Refrigerate.
2. Preheat the oven to 180°C (350°F/Gas 4). Brush 12 standard muffin holes with melted butter or oil. Cut the sheets of pastry into four equal squares and line each muffin hole with the pastry.
3. Bake for 15 minutes, or until golden. Place on a wire rack to cool and allow the puff pastry to settle. Using the back of a spoon, carefully push down the centre of the pastry to form a cup.
4. Combine the semi-frozen raspberries and icing sugar in a food processor and process until smooth. Pour the raspberry mixture into the cooled pastry cases.

banana bites

MAKES ABOUT 10

125 g (4 1/2 oz) milk chocolate, chopped

1 teaspoon oil

2 bananas, peeled and cut into 3 cm (1 1/4 inch) slices

95 g (3 1/4 oz/1/2 cup) chocolate sprinkles

1. Melt the chocolate in a bowl over hot water. Take off the heat. Add the oil and stir until smooth.
2. Spread the sprinkles on baking paper. Using a skewer, dip the banana into the chocolate, then roll in the sprinkles. Put on baking paper and leave to set. Serve on the skewers.

choc banana bites

MAKES 9

3 large bananas, peeled and cut into thirds

125 g (4 1/2 oz) dark chocolate, chopped

1. Line a large baking tray with foil. You need nine wooden ice-lolly sticks. Push a stick into each piece of banana. Put on the tray and freeze for 2 hours, or until firm.
2. Melt the chocolate in a bowl over hot water. Dip the banana pieces in the chocolate. Refrigerate until the chocolate has set, then wrap in plastic wrap and place in the freezer for at least 2 hours. Serve frozen.

frozen fruit kebabs

MAKES 4

140 g (5 oz) fresh pineapple

1/2 mango

80 g (2 3/4 oz) fresh seedless watermelon

100 g (3 1/2 oz) fresh rockmelon or any orange-fleshed melon

1. Remove the skin from all the fruit and cut into cubes or shapes.
2. You need four wooden ice-lolly sticks. Thread pieces of fruit onto each stick and freeze for 4 hours, or until frozen.
3. Remove from the freezer 10 minutes before eating to allow them to soften slightly.

fruity frozen yoghurt

MAKES 6

2 x 200 g (7 oz) tubs vanilla-flavoured yoghurt

170 g (6 oz) tinned passionfruit pulp in syrup

4 large strawberries, cut into small pieces

1 tablespoon icing (confectioners') sugar

1. Put the yoghurt, passionfruit and strawberries in a bowl.
2. Add the icing sugar and mix well.
3. Spoon into six glasses and freeze for 1 hour. Serve frozen.

squelch and crunch

MAKES 20

185 g (6½ oz) chocolate biscuits (cookies)
110 g (3¾ oz/½ cup) sugar
2 teaspoons gelatine powder
1 teaspoon vanilla extract
2–3 drops pink food colouring
coloured balls, to decorate

1. Line two baking trays with foil. Place the biscuits on the trays.
2. Combine the sugar, gelatine and 125 ml (4 fl oz/½ cup) of water in a saucepan. Stir over medium heat until the sugar dissolves and the mixture comes to the boil. Simmer, without stirring, for 4 minutes. Remove from the heat and cool.
3. Using electric beaters, beat the syrup for 5–6 minutes, or until the mixture is thick and glossy.
4. Add the vanilla and colouring and beat well. Spread a small amount to cover each biscuit. Smooth the surface and sprinkle with coloured balls.

swamp mud

SERVES 8

150 g (5½ oz) dark chocolate, chopped
4 eggs, separated
2 tablespoons caster (superfine) sugar
1 teaspoon grated orange zest
4 tablespoons cream
1 teaspoon gelatine powder
1 tablespoon orange juice
sprinkles, to decorate

1. Place the chocolate in a small heatproof bowl and sit it over a saucepan of simmering water. Stir until the chocolate has melted and the mixture is smooth. Cool slightly.
2. Using electric beaters, beat the egg yolks, sugar and zest in a large bowl for 5 minutes, or until thick and creamy. Beat in the cream and melted chocolate.
3. Combine the gelatine with the juice in a bowl. Stand the bowl in hot water and stir until the gelatine dissolves. Add to the chocolate mixture and beat until combined.
4. Place the egg whites in a clean, dry bowl. Using electric beaters, beat until firm peaks form. Add to the chocolate mixture. Fold in together until well combined. Refrigerate for 2 hours, or until set. Decorate with sprinkles.

choc-chip crackles

MAKES 24

90 g (3 1/4 oz/3 cups) puffed rice cereal

30 g (1 oz/1/4 cup) unsweetened cocoa powder

150 g (5 1/2 oz/1 1/4 cups) icing (confectioners') sugar

60 g (2 1/4 oz/1/2 cup) sultanas (golden raisins)

60 g (2 1/4 oz/2/3 cup) desiccated coconut

200 g (7 oz) Copha (white vegetable shortening), melted

50 g (1 3/4 oz/1/3 cup) dark chocolate chips

sprinkles, to decorate

1 Line 24 mini muffin holes with foil or double paper cases. Combine the puffed rice cereal, cocoa and sugar in a large bowl. Mix thoroughly, then stir in the sultanas and coconut. Stir in the melted shortening.

2 Spoon the mixture into the cases. Sprinkle with the chocolate chips and top with sprinkles. Refrigerate until set.

choc-cherry spiders

MAKES 20

100 g (3½ oz) glacé cherries, finely chopped
30 g (1 oz/⅓ cup) flaked almonds, toasted
100 g (3½ oz) packet fried egg noodles
200 g (7 oz) dark chocolate, chopped
30 g (1 oz) unsalted butter

1. Put the cherries in a bowl with the flaked almonds and noodles.
2. Melt the chocolate and butter in a small heatproof bowl over hot water. Stir until smooth.
3. Add the chocolate to the cherry mixture and stir gently to combine.
4. Put spoonfuls of the mixture onto a sheet of baking paper. Leave to set.

fairy wands

MAKES 10

125 g (4½ oz) unsalted butter, softened

115 g (4 oz/½ cup) caster (superfine) sugar

1 egg

250 g (9 oz/2 cups) plain (all-purpose) flour

200 g (7 oz) dark chocolate melts (buttons), melted

10 ice-lolly sticks

small silver balls, to decorate

1. Beat the butter, sugar and egg with electric beaters until creamy. Add the flour. Using your hands, press the mixture together to make a soft dough. Turn onto a lightly floured work surface and knead for 2 minutes, or until smooth. Cover with plastic wrap and put in the fridge for 30 minutes.
2. Preheat the oven to 180°C (350°F/Gas 4). Brush a large baking tray with melted butter or oil. Roll out the dough between sheets of baking paper to 5 mm (¼ inch) thick. Cut the dough into 20 stars using a star-shaped cutter. Arrange on the trays and bake for 15 minutes, or until golden. Cool on the trays.
3. Place ½ teaspoon of melted chocolate on the flat side of half the biscuits. Spread out to cover.
4. Attach the stick and sandwich the remaining biscuits over the chocolate and press together. Allow the chocolate to set.
5. Drizzle the remaining chocolate over the stars. Decorate with silver balls and allow to set.

pirate face biscuits

MAKES 30

250 g (9 oz/2 cups) icing (confectioners') sugar

1–2 tablespoons water

2–3 drops red food colouring

30 large plain round biscuits

4 liquorice straps

10 blue jellybeans, cut into 3

10 red jellybeans, cut into 3

15 black jellybeans, halved lengthways

1 Combine the icing sugar and water in a small bowl. Stand the bowl over a saucepan of simmering water and stir until smooth. Remove 1 tablespoon and tint with red food colouring, and set aside. Spread the biscuits evenly with the white icing.

2 Make the pirate faces while the icing is still wet. Cut the liquorice straps into semi-circles for the bandanna. Cut the licorice into strips for moustaches and any leftovers can be used for the eye patches. Use the jellybeans for the eye, mouth and patch. Make the dots on the bandanna using the red icing. Store the biscuits in the refrigerator until needed.

martian biscuits

MAKES 10

125 g (4½ oz) unsalted butter, softened

115 g (4 oz/½ cup) caster (superfine) sugar

1 egg

250 g (9 oz/2 cups) plain (all-purpose) flour

125 g (4½ oz/1 cup) icing (confectioners') sugar

3 tablespoons hot water

4 drops green food colouring

5 liquorice allsorts, thinly sliced

20 jellybeans, halved

5 jellys, cut into 4 pieces

1 To make the biscuits, beat the butter, sugar and egg with electric beaters until creamy. Add the flour.

2 Using your hands, press the mixture together to form a soft dough. Turn onto a lightly floured work surface and knead for 2 minutes, or until smooth. Cover with plastic wrap and refrigerate for 1 hour.

3 Preheat the oven to 180°C (350°F/Gas 4). Brush a large baking tray with melted butter or oil. Roll out the dough between sheets of baking paper to 5 mm (¼ inch) thick. Cut into shapes using gingerbread-people cutters. Put the biscuits on the tray and bake for 15 minutes, or until golden. Leave to cool.

4 Sift the icing sugar into a bowl. Add the water and food colouring and stir well. Dip the front of each biscuit into the icing. While the icing is still soft, decorate the biscuits, as shown, with the lollies.

teddy bear cakes

MAKES 12

340 g (12 oz) packet butter cake mix

100 g (3½ oz) dark chocolate chips

310 g (11 oz/1 cup) chocolate hazelnut spread

250 g (9 oz) honey-flavoured mini teddy biscuits

2 tablespoons sprinkles

1. Preheat the oven to 180°C (350°F/Gas 4). Lightly grease 12 standard muffin holes with oil.
2. Prepare the butter cake mix according to the directions on the packet. Fold the chocolate chips through the mixture.
3. Spoon the mixture into the prepared holes. Bake for 15 minutes, or until firm and golden brown. Allow to stand in the tin for 5 minutes. Remove the cakes and cool on a wire rack.
4. Spread each cake with the chocolate hazelnut spread. Place five teddy biscuits around the edge of the cakes. Decorate with sprinkles.

choc truffles

MAKES 24

50 g (1 3/4 oz) unsalted butter

4 tablespoons cream

250 g (9 oz) dark chocolate, chopped

100 g (3 1/2 oz) dark, milk or white chocolate, grated

1. Combine the butter and cream in a small saucepan. Stir over low heat until the butter has melted. Bring to the boil and remove from the heat immediately.
2. Place the chocolate in a heatproof bowl and pour in the hot cream mixture. Cover the bowl for about 1 minute and then stir until the chocolate has melted and the mixture is smooth. Cool in the refrigerator.
3. Roll heaped teaspoons into balls. Roll the balls in the grated chocolate. Place the truffles on a foil-lined baking tray and refrigerate until completely firm.

cactus juice

SERVES 8

1/2 Lebanese (short) cucumber, sliced

1 litre (35 fl oz/4 cups) apple juice

1 tablespoon honey

500 ml (17 fl oz/2 cups) chilled lemonade

500 ml (17 fl oz/2 cups) soda water

1 Place the cucumber in a large bowl with the apple juice and honey. Stir to combine. Cover and refrigerate for at least 1 hour.

2 Pour into eight glasses and add the lemonade and soda water. Top with ice cubes.

foaming craters

SERVES 8

250 g (9 oz) strawberries

8 scoops vanilla ice cream

lemonade, to serve

1 In a blender or food processor, process the strawberries until smooth.

2 Divide purée evenly among eight tall glasses.

3 Place a scoop of vanilla ice cream in each glass and top with lemonade, being careful not to overfill the glass. Serve immediately.

jungle juice

SERVES 8

850 ml (29 fl oz) unsweetened pineapple juice

750 ml (26 fl oz/3 cups) apple juice

450 g (1 lb) tinned unsweetened crushed pineapple

750 ml (26 fl oz/3 cups) chilled lemonade or dry ginger ale

glacé cherries, to garnish

1 Combine the pineapple juice, apple juice and crushed pineapple in a large bowl. Stir to combine. Cover and refrigerate for at least 1 hour.

2 Pour into eight glasses and add the lemonade or dry ginger ale. Garnish with cherries.

fruit punch

SERVES 10

125 ml (4 fl oz/1/2 cup) orange juice

425 g (15 oz) tinned fruit salad

juice of 1 orange

juice of 1 lemon

750 ml (26 fl oz/3 cups) chilled lemonade

fresh fruit, such as raspberries, blueberries, apple, orange, rockmelon and honeydew melon, to garnish

1 Combine the orange juice, fruit salad and the fresh orange and lemon juices in a bowl.

2 Stir lightly to combine. Cover and refrigerate for at least 1 hour.

3 Just before serving, add the lemonade. Garnish with fresh fruit.

pineapple cream

SERVES 2

450 g (1 lb) tinned undrained crushed pineapple

250 ml (9 fl oz/1 cup) pineapple juice

200 ml (7 fl oz) coconut milk

pineapple slices, to garnish

1. Combine the crushed pineapple and pineapple juice in a large bowl.
2. Slowly add the coconut milk, whisking continually until well blended.
3. To serve, pour into tall glasses over plenty of ice cubes. Garnish with pineapple slices. Serve immediately.

poison potion

SERVES 1

1 tablespoon lime cordial

1 tablespoon raspberry cordial

lemonade, to serve

1 scoop chocolate ice cream

1. Pour the lime and raspberry cordials into a large glass. Top with the lemonade.
2. Place the chocolate ice cream on top.
3. Allow to stand for 1 minute before serving.

choc-mint dream

MAKES 2

4 scoops choc-mint ice cream

375 ml (13 fl oz/1 1/2 cups) milk

chocolate sprinkles, to serve

1. Put 2 scoops of the ice cream and the milk in a blender and blend until smooth.
2. Pour into two tall glasses. Top each glass with a scoop of ice cream and chocolate sprinkles. Serve immediately.

pina colada

MAKES 2

375 ml (13 fl oz/1 1/2 cups) pineapple juice

1 banana

125 ml (4 fl oz/1/2 cup) tinned coconut milk

70 g (2 1/2 oz/1/2 cup) ice cubes (optional)

1. Put all the ingredients into a blender and blend until smooth.
2. Pour into two tall glasses to serve.

index

A

animal crisps 164
Anzac biscuits 132
apple and orange mini cakes 153
apples, baked 106
asparagus with parmesan 86

B

bananas
  banana bites 173
  banana and date fingers 156
  banana smoothie 34
  banana split 124
  upside-down banana cake 123
beach baby jellies 169
beef
  burger with the works 65
  lasagne 47
  mini burgers 159
  spaghetti bolognese 44
beer-battered fish and wedges 70
berries
  berry couscous 10
  berry froth 34
  berry muffins 12
  blood baths 170
  blueberry pancakes 14
  pear and raspberry crumble 102
  strawberry sauce 124
  strawberry shake 34
biscuits
  Anzac biscuits 132
  fairy wands 178
  gingerbread people 130
  jam drops 139
  martian biscuits 181
  melting moments 132
  pirate face biscuits 181
  squelch and crunch 174
bleeding fingers 170
blood baths 170
blueberry pancakes 14
bread and butter pudding 109
bubble and squeak 78
burger with the works 65

C

cactus juice 184
Caesar salad 87
cakes
  apple and orange mini cakes 153
  baby choc éclairs 167
  berry muffins 12
  carrot cake with ricotta topping 148
  chocolate cake 145
  cupcakes 151
  lemon butterfly cakes 152
  scones 146
  teddy bear cakes 182
  upside-down banana cake 123
capsicums, stuffed 99
caramel popcorn balls 164
caramel sauce 124
caramel slice 136
carrots
  carrot cake with ricotta topping 148
  honey carrots 95
cauliflower cheese 96

cheese
animal crisps 164
cauliflower cheese 96
cheesecakes, lemon 112
leek and cheese frittata 82
chicken
baked chicken nuggets 160
chicken and leek risotto 58
chicken noodle omelette 30
fresh spring rolls 26
orange and ginger chicken stir-fry 52
spaghetti with chicken meatballs 48
sticky chicken drumsticks 25
sweet chilli chicken and noodles 53
chilli
sweet chilli chicken and noodles 53
vegetarian chilli 77
Chinese vegetables, stir-fried 95
chocolate
baby choc éclairs 167
choc banana bites 173
choc truffles 183
choc-cherry spiders 177
choc-chip crackles 176
choc-honeycomb mousse 111
choc-mint dream 187
chocolate brownies 128
chocolate cake 145
chocolate chip cookies 129
hot choc sauce 124
swamp mud 174
coconut ice 142
corn fritters 33
cupcakes 151

D

dates
banana and date fingers 156
sticky date pudding 120
dhal 21
drinks
banana smoothie 34
berry froth 34
cactus juice 184
choc-mint dream 187
foaming craters 184
fresh fruit slushy 34
fruit punch 184
jungle juice 184
malted milkshake 37
mango whiz 37
moo juice 37
peach dream 37
pina colada 187
pineapple cream 187
poison potion 187
strawberry shake 34

E

éclairs, baby choc 167
eggs
chicken noodle omelette 30
corn fritters 33
leek and cheese frittata 82
scrambled eggs 17
enchiladas, tuna 74

F

fairy wands 178
fettucine carbonara 43
fish
beer-battered fish and wedges 70
fishcakes 73
tuna enchiladas 74
foaming craters 184
frankfurt bonbons 163
French toast 11
fried rice 66

fruit
fresh fruit slushy 34
frozen fruit kebabs 173
fruit jelly 110
fruit punch 184
fruity frozen yoghurt 173

G

gingerbread people 130
Greek salad 88
guacamole 21

H

ham and corn muffins 12
hash browns 90
honey carrots 95
hummus 18

J

jam drops 139
jam pudding 115
jelly
beach baby jellies 169
fruit jelly 110
jungle juice 184

L

lasagne 47
leek and cheese frittata 82
lemon butterfly cakes 152
lemon cheesecakes 112
lemon delicious 116
lime delicious, tangy 116

M

malted milkshake 37
mango whiz 37
martian biscuits 181
melting moments 132
meringue
bleeding fingers 170
meringues 147
pavlova 105
mini burgers 159
moo juice 37
muesli slice 135
mushrooms, stuffed 99

N

nachos 22
noodles
chicken noodle omelette 30
sweet chilli chicken and noodles 53
tofu with greens and noodles 81

O

orange and ginger chicken stir-fry 52

P

pancakes 119
blueberry 14
pasta
fettucine carbonara 43
lasagne 47
quick pasta with tomato sauce 43
spaghetti bolognese 44
spaghetti with chicken meatballs 48
spinach and ricotta cannelloni 57
pavlova 105
pea and ham risotto 58
peach dream 37
pear and raspberry crumble 102
pecan tarts 168
pina colada 187
pineapple cream 187

pirate face biscuits 181
pizza 40
poison potion 187
popcorn balls, caramel 164
pork
  pork and chive dumplings 61
  pork, pumpkin and cashew stir-fry 54
  san choy bau 51
potatoes
  baked potato wedges 160
  bubble and squeak 78
  fishcakes 73
  hash browns 90
  potato gnocchi with tomato sauce 69
  potato salad 92
  scalloped potatoes 92
pumpkin soup 29

R

raspberry crumble, pear and 102
ratatouille 91
rice
  chicken and leek risotto 58
  fried rice 66
  pea and ham risotto 58
rocky road 141

S

salads
  Caesar salad 87
  Greek salad 88
  mixed salad 88
  potato salad 92
san choy bau 51
sausages
  frankfurt bonbons 163
  sausage pie 62
scones 146
soup
  cream of tomato soup 29
  pumpkin soup 29
spaghetti bolognese 44
spaghetti with chicken meatballs 48
spinach and ricotta cannelloni 57
spring rolls, fresh 26
squelch and crunch 174
sticky date pudding 120
stir-fries
  orange and ginger chicken 52
  pork, pumpkin and cashew 54
  stir-fried Chinese vegetables 95
strawberry sauce 124
strawberry shake 34
swamp mud 174

T

teddy bear cakes 182
tofu with greens and noodles 81
tomatoes
  cream of tomato soup 29
  potato gnocchi with tomato sauce 69
  quick pasta with tomato sauce 43
  spinach and ricotta cannelloni 57
tuna enchiladas 74
tzatziki 18

V

vegetarian chilli 77
vegetables, stir-fried Chinese 95

Y

yoghurt, fruity frozen 173

Z

zebra sandwiches 156

This edition published in Canada in 2008 by Whitecap Books,
351 Lynn Ave., North Vancouver, British Columbia,
Canada, V7J 2C4
www.whitecap.ca

First published in 2007 by Murdoch Books Pty Limited
www.murdochbooks.com.au

Chief Executive: Juliet Rogers

Publishing Director: Kay Scarlett

Design Manager: Vivien Valk

Design concept, art direction and design: Alex Frampton

Project Manager: Jane Price

Editor: Gordana Trifunovic

Production: Maiya Levitch

Photographer: Michele Aboud

Stylist: Sarah DeNardi

Food preparation: Julie Ray and Simon Ruffell

© Text, design, photography and illustrations copyright 2007 Murdoch Books. All rights reserved. No part of this publication may be reproduced, stored in a retrieval system or transmitted in any form or by any means, electronic, mechanical, photocopying, recording or otherwise, without the prior written permission of the publisher.

ISBN 1 55285 890 1
ISBN 978 1 55285 890 5

Printed by C&C Offset Printing Co.Ltd in 2008. PRINTED IN CHINA.
Reprinted 2008.

The publisher and stylist would like to thank Typhoon, Rhubarb, French Bull by Jackie Shapiro, The Source, Villeroy & Boch, Marie Claire Paris plateware, Specklfarm Ribbons, Maxwell & Williams, Design Mode International and Spotlight for lending equipment for use and photography. Thank you to all the models: Felix, Ava, Ruby, Mia, Luca, Elena, Josie, Joe and Inez.

IMPORTANT: Those who might be at risk from the effects of salmonella poisoning (the elderly, pregnant women, young children and those suffering from immune deficiency diseases) should consult their doctor with any concerns about eating raw eggs.

CONVERSION GUIDE: You may find cooking times vary depending on the oven you are using. For fan-forced ovens, as a general rule, set the oven temperature to 20°C (35°F) lower than indicated in the recipe. We have used 20 ml (4 teaspoon) tablespoon measures. If you are using a 15 ml (3 teaspoon) tablespoon, for most recipes the difference will not be noticeable. However, for recipes using baking powder, gelatine, bicarbonate of soda (baking soda), small amounts of flour and cornflour (cornstarch), add an extra teaspoon for each tablespoon specified.